The Queen of Heaven

Bruce Bernard

The Queen of Heaven

A selection of paintings of the Virgin Mary *from the twelfth to the eighteenth centuries*

With an introductory essay by Peter Levi & notes to the Plates by Christopher Lloyd

Macdonald Orbis

A MACDONALD ORBIS BOOK
© Macdonald Orbis 1987
First published in Great Britain in 1987
by Macdonald & Co (Publishers) Ltd
London & Sydney

A member of BPCC plc

British Library Cataloguing in Publication Data
Bernard, Bruce
    Queen of Heaven
    1. Mary, *Mother of Jesus Christ*—Art
    2. Painting, European
    I. Title   II. Lloyd, Christopher, *1945—*
    755'.55   N8070

    ISBN 0-356-15044-5

Filmset in Monotype Poliphilus with Blado italic by
Balding + Mansell International Limited
Printed and bound in Italy by Graphicom SRL, Vicenza
Editors: Christopher Fagg, Mike Darton
Designer: Derek Birdsall

Picture acknowledgements

The author and publishers are grateful to the museums and
collections credited with each illustration for permission to
reproduce the paintings in this book. Photographs were supplied by
these collections with the exception of the following plates:

Artothek, Munich 42, 76, 100
Bildarchiv Preussischer Kulturbesitz, Berlin 5, 16, 58, 62, 78, 101
Lauros-Giraudon, Paris 95, 163
Magnum Photos/Eric Lessing, Paris 32, 80, 127
National Trust Photographic Library, London 155
Réunion des Musées Nationaux, Paris 29, 139
Scala, Florence 7, 10, 12, 14, 15, 18, 20, 21, 25, 36, 39, 46, 47, 52,
53, 54, 56, 57, 61, 64, 67, 74, 75, 77, 81, 82, 83, 85, 89, 92, 96, 97,
107, 112, 128, 132, 138, 140, 144, 147, 148, 149, 150, 152, 153,
154, 156, 158, 162, 164, 165,
Umberto Marzani, Milan 88

The scripture quotations in this publication are from the Revised
Standard Version of the Bible copyrighted 1946, 1952.
© 1971, 1973 by the Division of Christian Education of the
National Council of the Churches of Christ in the USA and used
by permission.

Contents

PREFACE

The idea for this book occurred to me while I was compiling a collection of biblical narrative paintings for what became *The Bible and its Painters*. At this time I saw so many painted images of the Virgin and Child that I thought it would be enjoyable and instructive to be able to compare the best of them in one book — and not only the most exalted ones, which it seemed to me would make a rather slimmer and less interesting volume. And I decided, as before, to restrict the choice to paintings on panel or canvas, with a few details of fresco, in the belief that the inclusion of drawings and manuscript illumination would weaken the concentration achieved if only works conceived to be on permanent view were shown.

Although I was brought up as a child to think of Mary as a figure related only to Christmas, I felt at quite an early age that she must be very near indeed to the centre of the Christian universe, and although my allegiance was never to the Catholic Church all other views of her seemed inadequate to me (perhaps I had glimpsed a picture). This book is therefore partly the expression of a sentiment that has never quite left me. It is even more about European art's extraordinary variety of response to the need to portray the Mother of God incarnate, its indispensable role in establishing her sway and the surprising freedom granted it in doing so.

It is only right that I should confess to some of the prejudices that have affected my choice of pictures where it may seem to demand an explanation. It will be quite obvious, for example, that I much prefer Giovanni Bellini's *Madonna of the Meadow* to Raphael's, as I have excluded the latter. The earlier of the two Raphaels that are in the book I chose for the character of the Madonna and not as a masterpiece. I admit that I find the fluency, ingenuity and often nakedly competitive spirit of the Highest Renaissance more and more irksome. I do not think, for example, that the section on the Annunciation suffers at all from Leonardo's absence or from that of Lorenzo Lotto's very clever picture. Much of the kind of painting that immediately followed in Italy I find at least as difficult to accept in terms of both form and sentiment, although through this book I have discovered Andrea del Sarto and become reconciled to Correggio and almost to the Caracci. I have not hesitated to include painters who can often seem rather improper like Lucas Cranach and Hans Baldung Grien, or some who have always struck me as somewhat repellent, like Jan Gossaert, because they have all given of their best to the Madonna. Van Orley, for instance, has contributed a wonderfully attractive picture, whereas his most famous altarpiece in Brussels has always seemed to me pointless and irritating. But all the tricks and perversities of the painters only serve to make the pure gold found in van Eyck, Bellini, Fra Angelico, Gerard David and Piero — as well as the real gold of the 14th century — shine even brighter.

Botticelli, too — even though the original choice of cover image for this book was an accidental one. Early in the book's production there was no image both suitable and available to make a sample cover from, but once printed it seemed almost impossible to consider any other. The way it combines what is close to what we know as glamour with the humour of the Christ Child finding his mother in a trance and unable to answer any of his questions, while yet remaining a sacred image, is one of the riddles that this collection sometimes poses. And when one looks at the scarf and make-up of the *Madonna of the Magnificat*, which seem the essence of twentieth-century chic, it is perhaps no wonder that the artist was soon asked to consider more closely the division of the sacred and profane. His great Lamentation (plate 147) shows that he did.

I make no apology for terminating the selection short of the nineteenth century and almost of the eighteenth. The pious German Nazarenes, their Scottish friend William Dyce and the Pre-Raphaelites, as well as Academicians or Salon painters brimming with sentiment, can now be seen to have been attempting a revival that in some way disobeyed the laws of art. Nowhere in the world could the subject of the Madonna be resuscitated, any more than could the Crucifixion or the Last Judgment. The Tiepolo reproduced (plate 136) tells us how the great painters began to fail the Madonna, however naturally possessive they felt or however brilliantly they applied the paint, and most of the picture sections in this book end with a picture that warns that the end is nigh — one section is even introduced by such a picture. The obsession of the late Baroque and Rococo with weightlessness seems to have robbed the subject of gravity of almost any kind. Surely Titian's Frari Assumption is as great as it is partly because Mary has retained enough of her earthly weight to suggest her essential humility; her apotheosis is not yet complete. Even on her Coronation she is more convincing when securely anchored.

One of the most interesting things about the images in this book is the difference between those from the north and south. In Italy the Madonna is generally idealized (or glamorized) however humble her origins are shown to have been. In the north she is often more like some plain unsistered Cinderella, gravely concentrating among the unaccustomed splendours that surround her when holding court or representing the Church on earth, and full of simple contentment when alone with her child. The enormous variety of expression with which different painters everywhere endow her, seems to prove that they were all working in the dark (except perhaps for St Luke), some of them with more clues than others and a very few even approaching the sheer wonder of the idea that brought her into being. Solemn, anxious, demure, good-humoured, homely, sometimes not all that bright, long-suffering in varying degrees and, at least once in this book, coolly to coldly appraising (as in Ribera's beautiful group with St Catherine), it may appear as if art is sometimes subjecting her to some sort of ordeal or even doubting her. And sometimes she responds with a subliminal impatience at the painter's presence. Of course she can come to no harm. The idea of a circle cannot be debased by drawing it inaccurately. But then her actual person is sometimes not of paramount importance. In one of the greatest painterly hymns of praise to her in this book, Bellini's San Zaccaria altarpiece, her face and figure are perhaps the least important part of the picture. It is the more than magical influence that she is unconsciously exerting on everything that surrounds her that matters. In her presence, saints meditate more patiently and profoundly. Music seems more deeply consoling and far beyond the pleasure principle. Ordinary architecture is transformed by a light that Bellini reserves for the Madonna alone, and even the air breathes like the element to which Gerard Manley Hopkins so eloquently compared her. She seems to be the essence of purest being and makes one understand that, however poignant effigies and carvings of her in wood and stone can be, it is only in painting that a sense of her total permeation of things can be experienced.

Painters in pursuit of the numinous today will certainly have to look elsewhere, whatever their faith. I am sure, however, that the contemplation of the pictures reproduced in this book will do no harm whatsoever to anyone, of whatever denomination, belief or prejudice — whether philosophical or aesthetic; my hope, indeed, is that it will have the very opposite effect.

Bruce Bernard

Introduction

Of all the religious and artistic images from the end of ancient Europe until the present twilight of Christianity, those of the Virgin Mary must surely be the most powerful and the most influential. But her meaning is not straightforward. It is multiple, and was so before the birth of Christ, in that there had already been a goddess or nymph as nursing mother in the Greek pantheon who could easily act as a model for the Virgin. Whatever may be true of theology, there is no doubt that religious images can change their meaning. The head of a broken statue of a Mycenean goddess was enshrined on a Greek island for centuries after it broke, apparently revered as the god Dionysos. The Christian Virgin is bride of God and mother of God and unwed girl, and the suffering woman of an epic, and heaven-queen with the moon under her feet, and Wisdom and the mystical Church, and plenty more; she personifies not an idea but whole complexes of ideas. She is more lowly and more glorified than a girl in a fairytale.

No doubt the feminists have been right in their analysis of some aspects of the cult of virginity. Even today the price put on virgins in certain marriage markets is high; finishing schools for the daughters of super-rich sheikhs are guarded by formidable dogs. But it is equally true that the image or symbol of the Virgin expresses something noble, imputing a special status to women that ended only with the rise of industrial society. An old Greek woman on a mountainside spinning the wool of her own sheep has more in common with medieval images of the Virgin than a woman factory worker because art draws on life, and art then drew on life then.

One must first understand history and society before one can know in what way or from what angle art or religion reflects them. Art idealizes and transmutes, and so does religion. By symbolizing the state of things, both help to make it permanent, as the feminist critics have pointed out, but art at least also opens up possibilities of a dreamlike multiplicity. A poem can hold contradictory ideas in co-existence and make harmony out of their tension, and visual art even more so.

It is essential to realize that, during the great period of European painting, the Virgin was not thought of as normal, not as everyday. She is at most half worldly, at least half other-worldly. The best pictures of her have the added mystery and ambiguity of all great art, as well as the self-contradictions of religion. Even in churches I think they are meant to attract admiration and wonder rather than prayer. For some psychological reason, a more archaic style of art is more expressive of divinity and touches religious feeling more deeply than realistic styles. The ancient Greeks noticed that about pre-classical statues of their gods, and it is certainly true of medieval statues of the Virgin. The Virgin in great art is wonderful and strange and above all beautiful, and one is not embarrassed to see her like that in a museum. Yet one feels distinctly uneasy to see some crudely carved, pregnant stone Virgin from an Irish church door placed in a museum, because its force as an image is not aesthetic but more direct.

Aesthetic delicacy has taken over the beautiful pictures, with no loss of power or dignity. The Virgin's qualities come and go from picture to picture, but her dignity and other-worldliness, as if she were a vision and her picture a revelation, are universal. Painting in the Renaissance was like a preview of the resurrection of the body: her body seems to have risen from the dead, her stillness is awe-inspiring, the beauty of her dress is unnatural. The angels in the Ferrarese Master's painting, with their black pointed wings and red pointed shoes, might have been raised up by some necromantic sage, in spite of their pious faces. She is the perfect mother of the one perfect child. She is doomed to see him die and to lament him dead; even Botticelli implies that with his delicate thorny wreath and his three nails. As a mother she concentrates uniquely on her child. And even when her effect is intended to be secondary, she still transforms everything else in the picture. To men and, I suppose, to women she is the supreme and protective mother.

I cannot follow the subtle logic of this relationship. As a boy I experienced it unselfconsciously, and I am sure the pretty Virgin with her colours and lights was a mother-substitute for normal Roman Catholic schoolboys. As I grew older and religion among other things took a sterner turn for me, I came to resent the beautiful Virgins of great art, probably because I was alarmed by their ambiguities, or resented the dominant side of my own mother, though I admit that I reserved an affection for the most magically beautiful early Renaissance Virgins, the most marriageable ones I fear. But in the end, as the sap of the youthful subconscious withered, there was little left I could take seriously as a religious image later than the twelfth century. It is only now and in the images of this book that I have turned back, and can revel in paradises that never were, miraculous Virgins unable to breathe, and the light, everlasting colours of great art.

History can never go backwards and we can never have another Renaissance. Nor will the status of women ever be precisely what it was. Recent images of the Virgin have been mostly part of pop art or commercial art. Even when the Virgin has appeared to innocent young people in the last hundred years, they have seen her in the expected terms that contemporary commercial art suggested. The same thing happened in the Roman Empire, when visions of the gods were determined by images of the gods that everyone could recognize. Since about 1700, the last occasional blossom of the Renaissance has been the freakish flowering of a dead bough; ideas about the Virgin have been over-simplified by being reduced to a sort of mad coherence, and her images in art have become coarsened. In so far as he is an exception to this sad process, Dali underlines the argument that there was always a surrealist element in painted images of the Virgin. Her proper poetry is the Spanish poetry of Gongora. When I think of Night in a Jewish poem like a negress in a star-embroidered robe, or the moon on her robe like the letter Yod, I think of the Virgin. She defies space: in the heaven of rococo painting reality is weightless.

The art of landscape painting has free play in the background of her portraits; much of the early history of landscape art in modern Europe is bound up with religious painting, particularly the birth of Christ, and the flight into Egypt. The first aesthetic ruins flourish in those same paintings, long before the suppression of the English or any other monasteries. Chaucer speaks of the broken silence and the broken cloister of her breast. It must be said that the image of the Virgin and Child carries among other meanings some sense of wonder at the consequences of the act of sex: she is a cosmic symbol of life, and the landscape around her or below her is no more than the familiar fields over which she chooses or accepts to reign. The Cambridge-blue Italian sky is dawn, I suppose: anyway, it adds to the giddy sensation of lightness and surprise.

Pictures of the Virgin had a curious frankness. Personal portraits of women were smug by comparison, and often communicated little beyond social rank. The Virgin is a figure of perfect drawing and pure fantasy. The target had been set by early masters, and included originality because the painting must arouse awe, part of its effect being stunning surprise, another part reverence, another admiration of unexpected details, the whole composition at the same time being luminous, harmonious, formality disguised as informality, heaven disguised as earth.

The Virgin is perfectly beautiful, and as kind-looking as any young mother at the school gates. She almost never looks like a nun, she is not unapproachable, but posed, frozen, alive only because some inward trance or spring of life sustains her. The Child, of course, is even less realistic. God he may be, but he is only her attribute, and her halo is bigger than his.

In those paintings into which more realism enters, the effect is thrilling because ageing and suffering become real. The most striking of all examples is Bruegel's *Death of the Virgin*, in which the apostles stare as they crowd around, and are certainly awe-stricken. This is an early masterpiece involving the play of light in a dark room.

One might imagine it had been painted in shades of ochre on specially ancient yellow paper, and yet inside it the tip of a candle blazes. The great Rembrandt could hardly have done better. The woman who has fallen asleep by the fire really does look worn out. Is she a touch of realism for its own sake, or was she a poor servant, unworthy to watch the death which only the apostles witnessed? Was it unthinkable to have a woman's deathbed surrounded by men without another woman present? The old woman dying, and the old apostle peering, form an unforgettable image. The bedcurtain like a black thundercloud makes it more frightening.

I find it odd that so far as I know there are no poems, at least in English, to come near these pictures. The medieval Latin poems are just like the famous Middle English lyric sung as a Christmas hymn, *I Sing of a Maiden*. They are fresh and moving in their way, but they do not begin to approach the mysterious mutual interplay of the painted images. Moses sees the Virgin in the Burning Bush, where he ought only to recognize God. The bush itself is not a thorn tree in the desert, but a robust green tree, full of delights. Renaissance Latin poetry about the Virgin was certainly written, though scarcely in England, but even Milton's master Sannazaro never attains the complexity of such pictures. The painters comment on one another and on their personal themes and on their subject, independently of poetry. The prose mythology of the Virgin, and the jumble of Biblical texts that are attached to her, are meagre-looking sources to have produced such wealth.

In the Tarot pack the likeness of Il Mondo to the Virgin emboldens me to suggest there is something archetypal and profoundly, subconsciously stirring in the image of the Virgin and Child. I don't think it stands only for psychological sterility or the suppression of women's desires, though I see how both meanings can attach to it. In England the Virgin Diana of the woods and of Latin poetry came after, not before, the Christian Virgin and was a substitute for her in painting and in English verse. Possibly at the bottom of the whole box of tricks lies the imagined relation of the moon with the sun: there is often something blood-chilling and lunar about paintings of the Virgin, though one also notices a tranquil and ecstatic warmth, an ecstasy that is not passionate. Her eyes are sibyl's eyes, but a modest, self-contained sibyl.

These are not images that do anything: you cannot even dress them up or crown them like the doll-like Virgins venerated in Spain. As Auden said of poetry, they bring nothing about. They are pure art, not religious contemplation, but an inspiring invasion of the sacred by that secular part of the soul we call imagination. Imagination, having once entered the closed world of the sacred, wanders about musing like Alice in Wonderland. These images are very deeply and thoroughly imagined. Icons that do wonders like the one at Venice which brought victory at Lepanto, or the Virgin of Vladimir that was fought for, have blunter features. In developed Western painting it is the icon itself that is intended to be the wonder.

Maybe there are so many, or we are so familiar with some of them, that now no image moves us more than the others, and we are struck only by the simplest, no longer by the most extreme. I have passed through that mood, as I said, and returned to seeing each one as an individual work of art. Each one creates and organizes its individual, pictorial space. They hint at wisdom of very different kinds, and at different beliefs about space and about the stars, now and then even at different kinds of geometry. It is as if there were no more a shared Virgin between artists than there can be a shared dream. The invisible barrier between these artists and ourselves is not difference of belief, or not in my own case, but the conception they share as a final consequence of the Renaissance that anything whatsoever can be skilfully represented, including the invisible and the spiritual. Today our visions are much wilder, and we are inclined to think almost nothing can be adequately represented.

When did beliefs about the Virgin become impossible to represent? The feminists are right to point to the grotesque consequences of insisting on a detailed definition of what virginity means in the first place, and the absurdity of failing to do so. The bodily parts of women were presumably more of a mystery to the medieval clergy than the way an angel would dress. But apart from that crucial area, everything about the Virgin was solidly imaginable. The Immaculate Conception, the doctrine that she was sinless, a new creation outside the normal run of human beings is mysterious and abstract, but it can be symbolized, and it helps to account for her unearthly look in painting. The doctrine of her bodily Assumption into heaven, a sort of replay or initiation of Christ's Ascension, has a rococo effect in art, but the image is clear enough. It was proclaimed as a dogma of the Church by Pius XII only in 1950, long after the classic days of the image, but Robert Lowell fixed the moment unforgettably:

> *When Pius the Twelfth made Mary's Assumption dogma,*
> *She soared up like a gorgeous jungle bird*
> *Outmarvelling the miracles of science.*
> *The costumed Switzers sloped their pikes to push*
> *(O Pius) through the monstrous human crush;*
> *God herded his people to the* coup de grâce.

These images are more extreme than any to be found within the catalogue of great paintings; even El Greco exploding away into fireworks is intellectually less violent. The avalanche of extreme imagination of religious scenes has got beyond what was possible in Renaissance art. When Blake drew the Virgin he was conservative, because he well understood the convention in which she belonged, even though in his day it was dying. For El Greco the Virgin was transfigured in a kind of transformation scene between two worlds, because his own painting as he drew her was being transformed between two cultures. The bearded stars glistening on the Virgin's shoulder in the Botticelli painting indicate holy astrology, which is another dimension of meaning, but they remain at home in the same world of his art, however many cultures that included or transcended.

Within her paintings, the Virgin is among other things the individual soul gazing at God, a God to whom she has given birth. She is the soul of Socrates contemplating the beautiful and true. This neoplatonist idea is so common in the Renaissance that one would be surprised if it had failed to penetrate religious art. But all that the person seeing the picture recognizes is what the soul recognizes of itself, some kind of outer hem of the beautiful, and an aspect of truth like a moment caught from time. I hope these sentences will not seem pretentious or obscure: I feel bound to write them as the nearest approach I can make to the way the painters expected their work to be regarded — apart, that is, from what is written in the Christian scriptures.

When the Bible ceased to hang like a millstone round most people's necks, about two generations ago, people made more than one effort to rescue it for literature. One of the reasons they were largely unsuccessful is that 'the Bible as literature' is somehow the Bible emasculated. One has to read it as scripture whether one believes it or not, with few exceptions such as the *Song of Solomon*. There is a similar catch about admiring or loving pictures of the Virgin purely as 'works of art'. There is nothing pure about a work of art, least of all its form. Pictures of the Virgin are never as secular as they may look. They are usually painted for churches as part of an immortal monument, to embody a central truth about the providence of God. The story of the Virgin, if it is traced without prejudice, is very beautiful, and so are the paintings. Their mystery is physical, because they are the work of human hands, but it is not quite secular, it is sacred, and in many ways and at many levels conveys intimate meaning. One must make at least as strong a gesture of imaginative sympathy towards this art as one would do towards Greek statues or Egyptian paintings; otherwise one is lost.

Doctrine is a process that ramifies slowly from a simple origin. The doctrines incorporating the Virgin as an image and a personality developed early, though their remoter consequences ossified into doctrines much later. If Christ was God and son of God, then his birth was unearthly and his mother specially chosen by God. That had become clear in the first centuries of Christianity.

Her own peculiar purity from the moment of her own conception, which mysteriously exempts her from the consequences of the 'original sin' of Adam and Eve, is a remote consequence of this early doctrine. The dogma of the Immaculate Conception (of the Virgin, not of Christ) was defined as a dogma only in the atmosphere of hothouse piety that was generated in the nineteenth century. Her bodily Assumption into heaven without death, a view favoured by Pius XII but contrary to the Greek and Russian Orthodox belief that she first died and then rose up, is the direct consequence of her not being subject to 'original sin' for which the human race was punished by death. All these doctrines were considered in the earliest Middle Ages; they became rigid dogmas only when the Church itself had become defiant and rigid.

I doubt whether the later history of art as it touches the Virgin is much affected by exaggerations of belief. She certainly became less real, and floated away into a heaven more unreal still. By the end of the Middle Ages she was the mother of us all, the one person through whom we approached the supreme power. In Michelangelo's *Last Judgment*, she could not bear to see damnation and turned away her eyes. There are analogies of these attitudes both in the family and in the state. But the images of the Virgin by 1700 are more affected by art history and by real history than by doctrine. The elements of thought about her that coexisted in the Renaissance no longer came together in her pictures. The Renaissance was over.

The Renaissance is variously defined and variously dated, yet it is an oddly single period and process in some ways. These Virgins come close to its essential nature. That would allow it to begin with Dante, as people often say that it did. In Dante's lifework, everything seems to lead to the image of the Virgin. Typically of the Renaissance, the final image is both complex and direct. The last canto of the *Paradiso* is as dateless and permanent as are the paintings: 'Vergine madre, figlia del tuo figlio . . . who so ennobled human flesh that your maker did not scorn to be your making.' That is more or less what all these pictures are saying in their very different ways. The sense of human dignity lies at the heart of the Renaissance from beginning to end.

For myself I am never quite sure whether I prefer the most traditional images of the Virgin or the most unexpected. The Annunciation is always a good subject. It has an abstract relation to human courtship, like that of a very formal dance. The lily in the angel's hand, which survives here and there in England in the public-house name, the Pot of Flowers, is both earthly and unearthly, as the Virgin is. In Romano's painting, the greenish-gold background adds sufficiently to the mystery to make God in his pigeon-loft and the Holy Spirit in flight just as acceptable as the realistic dowry bags the Virgin is handing out to the little girls. Even the superhuman scale of the principal figures is acceptable, because their colours echo one another, and we already know what to expect of them. The angel salutes, the Virgin submits, God blesses, as they have done on a thousand earlier canvases. So the Virgin leaning over at the moment of Annunciation to give her prizes to the little girls is a special miracle because it departs from the norm. If the four modern figures were lifesize they would be a shocking interruption and the picture would be absurd. As it is, I am fond of it; it is both traditional and something quite new that occurs very late in the tradition. One of the great discoveries of this book is Gentileschi, and the same is true of him, his daring being matched only by his restraint.

Of the pictures collected here, those from the Renaissance are painted to catch the eye, and then to hold it entranced, and now they have taken on the added charm and difficulty of belonging to a world that has quite evaporated. They were made to give pleasure, of an innocent intensity about which we can only speculate because we are too doubtful, too knowing, and too ashamed of ourselves. They are holy objects from a world in which such things were numerous and normal. Their zest and realism about the Virgin, about angels and God and the host and about the distant landscape, indicate a confidence we can scarcely recapture. They were not meant to overwhelm you with their patina of antiquity, but to amaze you by their modernity, the freshness of the brush-strokes.

Peter Levi
June 1987

The Icon & the Byzantine Tradition

The word icon used in the broadest sense means literally 'image', but more specifically today it refers to a religious image inspiring special veneration. It is overwhelmingly associated with the Byzantine Christian tradition which emerged in the Greek-speaking eastern Roman Empire during the fourth and fifth centuries, and was later established as the Orthodox Church. The eastern capital, Constantinople, founded by the Emperor Constantine on the site of ancient Byzantium, was the 'second Rome', bearing a spiritual primacy to the Eastern Rite similar to that later exercised by Rome over the Latin Rite.

The most common form of icon is that painted on wood, but several other types of varying sizes and formats are known, including those executed in mosaic, precious metals and ivory. The earliest painted icons were executed in a thick wax-like medium known as encaustic, but tempera was also used and eventually replaced encaustic. A limited number of icons dating from the sixth to the tenth century have survived and the study of the stylistic development of icon painting only tentatively begins during the eleventh and twelfth centuries. The incidence of survival is greater for the thirteenth century and after. The compositions and subject-matter of icons are strictly traditional, and as a result many icons can look deceptively early in date. This almost entirely separates them in character from the majority of pictures shown in this book and is underlined by the fundamental change in El Greco's art when he crossed over traditions to take part in the constantly developing vision of the European Renaissance.

The visual origins of the icon may be traced from sources as diverse as Egyptian mummy portraits, representations of the emperors made as part of the Roman imperial cult, and pagan religious rites. With the rise of Christianity and the establishment of the Orthodox Church the icon began to play a major role in the liturgy, particularly in the commemoration of feast days and saints' days. From being an object originally used in the context of private worship, the icon eventually began to be accepted as a standard part of church furnishings. Soon there were so many that it became necessary to hang them on a screen (called the iconostasis) separating the sanctuary from the nave. The veneration of images has never been so widely accepted in the Latin West, but even in the Orthodox Church it was a disputed matter that reached a climax during the eighth century with the controversy known as Iconoclasm. Those who defended the use of icons emphasized that it was not the object itself that was being worshipped, but 'the prototype behind the image which became manifest through representation' (Weitzmann). The need for imagery as an agent in the act of worship regained official acceptance during the ninth century and the cult of the icon increased. Eventually, icons came to be produced throughout the Orthodox world, from Greece and the Balkans to Russia and the Near East. The influence of icons and icon painters can also be felt in European art, as in the Pisan example shown overleaf, particularly during the thirteenth century when contacts established through trade and the various crusades led to a westward flow of objects and an interchange of ideas if not also of skills. Even after the fall of Constantinople in 1453 the art of icon painting found an alternative outlet in Crete until at least the sixteenth and even the seventeenth centuries.

I
RUSSIAN SCHOOL (twelfth century)
The Virgin of the Great Panagia
(called *The Virgin Orant of Yaroslavl*)
192 × 122 cm, Tretyakov Gallery, Moscow

2
MASTER OF SS. COSMAS AND DAMIAN
(Pisan school, 1265–1285)
The Virgin and Child
64 × 44 cm, Fogg Art Museum,
Harvard University, Cambridge (Mass.).
Friends of the Fogg Art Museum Fund

3
EL GRECO (DOMENIKOS THEOTOKOPOULOS)
(1541–1614)
St Luke Painting the Virgin and Child
42 × 33 cm, Benaki Museum, Athens

The Apocryphal Life of the Virgin

There have been many more stories told about the Virgin Mary outside the New Testament than within it. They come from a body of texts of which a few are roughly contemporary with the Gospels, while others were written up to five hundred years later; in addition there was a strong oral tradition. The currency and persistence of these legends and stories arose from the very natural desire to supplement the scanty information about the Virgin provided in the scriptures and the need for the Church itself to confirm the complete sanctity of the origins and nature of Christ's mother.

The account of her immediate antecedents served to show that her selection as the mother of the son of God was divinely planned and that she was not chosen by reason of ordinary virtue. The story of her parents, Joachim and Anna, is told in paintings by Giotto among many others, and a complex family tree was established. According to the version current in the early fourteenth century Mary was miraculously conceived following the chaste embrace of her parents by the Golden Gate in Jerusalem. This story gave rise to the doctrine of the Immaculate Conception, a subject treated allegorically by a number of painters and, as in the Velázquez overleaf, she is generally shown in space with the moon at her feet and the sun behind her. There are also charming pictures of her natural birth, often attended by angels (plate 5). The splendid Titian (plate 7) shows Mary being received into the Temple, a scene which both underlines and emblematizes the saintliness of her youth in the apocryphal accounts.

From conception, birth and youth, the story of Mary's life moves to her marriage, the preliminaries to which are again attended by the miraculous. Bachelors and widowers competed for her hand by leaving their wooden staffs by her house overnight in hopes that a miraculous sprouting of leaves would single out the staff of the successful suitor. Joseph's staff it was that blossomed; and so he and Mary became man and wife.

With the Nativity we return to the scriptural account. But even here the gospel story of Mary became embroidered with imaginary and intriguing detail. The Flight into Egypt, for example, is especially rich in incident in the popular accounts on which the Renaissance painters drew for imagery: pagan idols fall at the approach of the Holy Family, trees miraculously bend down to offer the travellers their fruit, and cornfields spring up in which they hide from Herod's soldiers.

As Christ's life on earth nears its tragic climax, the apocryphal — though not the scriptural — tradition places Mary at crucial episodes. She is sometimes depicted as taking leave of Christ before his final entry into Jerusalem, as in the touching portrayal by Gerard David (plate 6). But it is the imagery of the scenes immediately following the Crucifixion which inspired some of the greatest art that has Mary as its focus. In the gospel narrative she leaves the scene of the Crucifixion and is not present at the Deposition or the Entombment. But the Pietà, the image of Mary mourning over the dead body of her son, has a power — as can be seen in this collection — which puts it beyond any necessary connection to biblical text. She is often also portrayed as being present at the Ascension and with the disciples at the Feast of Pentecost.

These imaginary, or rather imagined, scenes from the life of the Virgin did not exclude the manner of her own death. The doctrine of the Assumption (though not finally confirmed until 1950 by Pope Pius XII) arose from the proposition that, if free from all sin, Mary could not have died like an ordinary human being. A legend tells of the Apostles making a pilgrimage to attend her last illness; according to one tradition, they find only flowers in her tomb; according to another they see her die and, on her interment, see her drawn up to heaven. On her arrival there, it seemed only natural that she should be crowned Queen.

4
DIEGO VELÁZQUEZ (1599–1660)
The Virgin of the Immaculate Conception
134.6 × 101.6 cm, National Gallery, London

5
MAIR VON LANDSHUT (active c.1485–1510)
The Birth of the Virgin
38 × 31 cm, Gemäldegalerie Staatliche Museen
Preussischer Kulturbesitz, Berlin

6
GERARD DAVID (c.1460–1523)
Christ taking leave of his Mother
15.6 × 12.1 cm, The Metropolitan Museum of Art,
New York. Bequest of Benjamin Altman

7
TITIAN (TIZIANO VECELLIO) (*c.*1477–1576)
The Presentation of the Virgin
335 × 775 cm, Galleria dell' Accademia, Venice

The Annunciation

In the sixth month the angel Gabriel was sent from God to a city of Galilee named Nazareth, to a virgin betrothed to a man whose name was Joseph, of the house of David; and the virgin's name was Mary. And he came to her and said, 'Hail, O favoured one, the Lord is with you!' But she was greatly troubled at the saying, and considered in her mind what sort of greeting this might be. And the angel said to her, 'Do not be afraid, Mary, for you have found favour with God. And behold, you will conceive in your womb and bear a son, and you shall call his name Jesus. He will be great, and will be called the Son of the Most High; and the Lord God will give to him the throne of his father David, and he will reign over the house of Jacob for ever; and of his kingdom there will be no end.' And Mary said to the angel, 'How shall this be, since I have no husband?' And the angel said to her, 'The Holy Spirit will come upon you, and the power of the Most High will overshadow you; therefore the child to be born will be called holy, the Son of God. And behold, your kinswoman Elizabeth in her old age has also conceived a son; and this is the sixth month with her who was called barren. For with God nothing will be impossible.' And Mary said, 'Behold, I am the handmaid of the Lord; let it be to me according to your word.' And the angel departed from her.

LUKE Chapter 1, Verses 26–38

8
SIMONE MARTINI (c.1284–1344)
The Annunciation
184 × 114 cm (centre); 105 × 48 cm (each side
panel), Galleria degli Uffizi, Florence

9
JAN VAN EYCK (active 1422–1441)
The Annunciation
each 39 × 24 cm, Thyssen-Bornemisza
Collection, Lugano

10
FRA ANGELICO (c.1395–1455)
The Annunciation
194 × 194 cm, Museo del Prado, Madrid

11
ATTRIBUTED TO JAN VAN EYCK (active 1422–1441)
The Annunciation
77.5 × 64.5 cm, The Metropolitan Museum of Art,
New York. Bequest of Michael Friedsam,
The Friedsam Collection

12
PIERO DELLA FRANCESCA (*c*.1416–1492)
The Annunciation
329 × 193 cm, San Francesco, Arezzo

13
CARLO CRIVELLI (active 1457–1493)
The Annunciation with St Emidius
207 × 146.5 cm, National Gallery, London

OPVS CARO
LI · CRIVELLI ·
VENETI ·

1486

14
SANDRO BOTTICELLI (1445–1510)
The Annunciation
150 × 156 cm, Galleria degli Uffizi, Florence

15
LORENZO DI CREDI (1456–1536)
The Annunciation
88 × 71 cm, Galleria degli Uffizi, Florence

16
GAUDENZIO FERRARI (1475/85–1546)
The Annunciation
88 × 86 cm, Gemäldegalerie Staatliche Museen
Preussischer Kulturbesitz, Berlin

17
ANTONIAZZO ROMANO (IL CATALANO)
(documented 1461–1510)
The Annunciation
Santa Maria sopra Minerva, Rome

18
ORAZIO GENTILESCHI (1562–1647)
The Annunciation
289 × 198 cm, Galleria Sabauda, Turin

19
CORNELIS VAN POELENBURGH (*c.*1586–1667)
The Annunciation
48 × 41 cm, Kunsthistorisches Museum, Vienna

The Nativity & the Holy Family

In those days a decree went out from Caesar Augustus that all the world should be enrolled. This was the first enrolment, when Quirinius was governor of Syria. And all went to be enrolled, each to his own city. And Joseph also went up from Galilee, from the city of Nazareth, to Judea, to the city of David, which is called Bethlehem, because he was of the house and lineage of David, to be enrolled with Mary, his betrothed, who was with child. And while they were there, the time came for her to be delivered. And she gave birth to her first-born son and wrapped him in swaddling cloths, and laid him in a manger, because there was no place for them in the inn.

And in that region there were shepherds out in the field, keeping watch over their flock by night. And an angel of the Lord appeared to them, and the glory of the Lord shone around them, and they were filled with fear. And the angel said to them, 'Be not afraid; for behold, I bring you good news of a great joy which will come to all the people; for to you is born this day in the city of David a Saviour, who is Christ the Lord. And this will be a sign for you: you will find a babe wrapped in swaddling cloths and lying in a manger.' And suddenly there was with the angel a multitude of the heavenly host praising God and saying, 'Glory to God in the highest, and on earth peace among men with whom he is pleased!'

When the angels went away from them into heaven, the shepherds said to one another, 'Let us go over to Bethlehem and see this thing that has happened, which the Lord has made known to us.' And they went with haste, and found Mary and Joseph, and the babe lying in a manger.

LUKE Chapter 2, Verses 1–16

20
PIERO DELLA FRANCESCA (c.1416–1492)
Madonna del Parto
260 × 203 cm, Chapel of the Cemetery, Monterchi

21
HUGO VAN DER GOES (c.1440–1482)
The Adoration of the Shepherds
249 × 300 cm, Galleria degli Uffizi, Florence

22
FILIPPINO LIPPI (c.1457–1504)
The Nativity with two Angels
25 × 37 cm, National Gallery of Scotland, Edinburgh

23
FOLLOWER OF JAN JOEST VAN CALCAR
(*c*.1455/60–1519)
The Nativity
101 × 70 cm, The Metropolitan Museum of Art,
New York: the Jack and Belle Linsky Collection

24
GEERTGEN TOT SINT JANS (*c*.1455/65–1485/95)
The Nativity at Night
34 × 25 cm, National Gallery, London

25
JACOPO TINTORETTO (1518–1594)
The Nativity
542 × 455 cm, Scuola di San Rocco, Venice

26
PETRUS CHRISTUS (*c*.1410–1472/3)
The Virgin and Child in a Gothic Interior
69.5 × 58 cm, The Nelson-Atkins Museum of Art,
Kansas City. Nelson Fund

27
MASTER OF THE MAGDALEN LEGEND
(c.1483–1527)
The Holy Family
65 × 52 cm, Koninklijk Museum voor Schone
Kunsten, Antwerp

28
PETER PAUL RUBENS (1577–1640)
*The Holy Family under the Apple Tree with S.S. John
the Baptist, Elizabeth and Zacharias*
353 × 233 cm, Kunsthistorisches Museum, Vienna

29
REMBRANDT VAN RIJN (1606–1669)
The Holy Family
41 × 34 cm, Musée du Louvre, Paris

30
PIETER FRANSZ DE GREBBER (*c.*1600–1652/3)
The Virgin Teaching the Christ Child to Read
95.5 × 74 cm, Musée des Beaux-Arts, Quimper

The Magi

Now when Jesus was born in Bethlehem of Judea in the days of Herod the king, behold, wise men from the East came to Jerusalem, saying, 'Where is he who has been born king of the Jews? For we have seen his star in the East, and have come to worship him.' When Herod the king heard this, he was troubled, and all Jerusalem with him; and assembling all the chief priests and scribes of the people, he inquired of them where the Christ was to be born. They told him, 'In Bethlehem of Judea; for so it is written by the prophet: "And you, O Bethlehem, in the land of Judah, are by no means least among the rulers of Judah; for from you shall come a ruler who will govern my people Israel."'

31
GIOTTO DI BONDONE (1276–1337)
The Epiphany
44.9 × 43.7 cm, The Metropolitan Museum of Art,
New York. John Stewart Kennedy Fund

32
THEODORIC (active mid-fourteenth century)
The Adoration of the Kings (detail)
Kreuzkappelle, Karlštejn Castle

33
MASTER OF LIESBORN (active second half of the
fifteenth century)
The Adoration of the Child and The Adoration of the Kings
each 58.5 × 37.5 cm, Westfälisches Landesmuseum
für Kunst und Kulturgeschichte, Münster

34
PETER PAUL RUBENS (1577–1640)
The Adoration of the Kings
447 × 336 cm, Koninklijk Museum voor Schone
Kunsten, Antwerp

35
JEAN-HONORÉ FRAGONARD (1732–1806)
The Rest on the Flight into Egypt
67 × 57 cm, Baltimore Museum of Art: the Mary
Frick Jacobs Collection

The Flight into Egypt

Then Herod summoned the wise men secretly and ascertained from them what time the star appeared; and he sent them to Bethlehem, saying, 'Go and search diligently for the child, and when you have found him bring me word, that I too may come and worship him.' When they had heard the king they went their way; and lo, the star which they had seen in the East went before them, till it came to rest over the place where the child was. When they saw the star, they rejoiced exceedingly with great joy; and going into the house they saw the child with Mary his mother, and they fell down and worshipped him. Then, opening their treasures, they offered him gifts, gold and frankincense and myrrh. And being warned in a dream not to return to Herod, they departed to their own country by another way.

Now when they had departed, behold, an angel of the Lord appeared to Joseph in a dream and said, 'Rise, take the child and his mother, and flee to Egypt, and remain there till I tell you; for Herod is about to search for the child, to destroy him.' And he rose and took the child and his mother by night, and departed to Egypt, and remained there until the death of Herod. This was to fulfil what the Lord had spoken by the prophet, 'Out of Egypt have I called my son.'

Then Herod, when he saw that he had been tricked by the wise men, was in a furious rage, and he sent and killed all the male children in Bethlehem and in all that region who were two years old or under, according to the time which he had ascertained from the wise men. Then was fulfilled what was spoken by the prophet Jeremiah: 'A voice was heard in Ramah, wailing and loud lamentation, Rachel weeping for her children; she refused to be consoled, because they were no more.'

MATTHEW Chapter 2, Verses 1–18

36
GIOTTO DI BONDONE (1276–1337)
The Flight into Egypt
200 × 185 cm, Capella degli Scrovegni (Arena
Chapel), Padua

37
VITTORE CARPACCIO (*c.*1460–1523/6)
The Flight into Egypt
72 × 111.5 cm, National Gallery of Art,
Washington D.C.: the Andrew W. Mellon
Collection

38

JOOS VAN CLEVE (c.1464–1540)
The Rest on the Flight into Egypt
54 × 67.5 cm, Musées Royaux des Beaux-Arts,
Brussels

39
JOACHIM PATINIR (*c*.1485–1524)
The Rest on the Flight into Egypt
121 × 177 cm, Museo del Prado, Madrid

40
GERARD DAVID (c.1460–1523)
The Rest on the Flight into Egypt
44.3 × 44.9 cm, National Gallery of Art,
Washington D.C.: the Andrew W. Mellon
Collection

41
ORAZIO GENTILESCHI (1562–1647)
The Rest on the Flight into Egypt
175.3 × 218.4 cm,
Birmingham Museums and Art Gallery

42
ANTHONY VAN DYCK (1599–1641)
The Rest on the Flight into Egypt
134.5 × 114.5 cm, Alte Pinakothek, Munich

43
ADRIAEN VAN DER WERFF (1659–1722)
The Rest on the Flight into Egypt
54.5 × 43 cm, National Gallery, London

The Presentation & Circumcision

And when the time came for their purification according to the law of Moses, they brought him up to Jerusalem to present him to the Lord (as it is written in the law of the Lord, 'Every male that opens the womb shall be called holy to the Lord').

LUKE Chapter 2, Verses 22–23

And at the end of eight days, when he was circumcised, he was called Jesus, the name given by the angel before he was conceived in the womb.

LUKE Chapter 2, Verse 21

44
ANDREA MANTEGNA (1430/1–1506)
The Presentation of Christ in the Temple
69 × 86.3 cm, Gemäldegalerie Staatliche Museen
Preussischer Kulturbesitz, Berlin

45

GIOVANNI BELLINI (c.1430–1516)
The Circumcision
75 × 102 cm, National Gallery, London

The Madonna & Child

46
CIMABUE (CENNI DI PEPPI) (c.1240–after 1302)
The Virgin and Child Enthroned, Surrounded by Angels
427 × 280 cm, Musée du Louvre, Paris

47
DUCCIO DI BUONINSEGNA (active 1278–1318/19)
The Virgin and Child with two Angels
89 × 60 cm, Museo dell' Opera della Metropolitana,
Siena

48
TADDEO DI BARTOLO (c.1362–1422)
Head of the Virgin
19.7 × 13.7 cm, The Metropolitan Museum of Art,
New York: the Robert Lehman Collection

49
TADDEO DI BARTOLO (c.1362–1422)
The Virgin and Child
100.3 × 68 cm, Philbrook Art Center, Tulsa

50

MASTER OF THE ST VERDIANA PANEL (active
c.1390—1415)
The Virgin and Child with Saints
80.7 × 54.3 cm, High Museum of Art, Atlanta.
Gift of the Samuel H. Kress Foundation

51
GENTILE DA FABRIANO (*c*.1370–1427)
The Virgin and Child with SS. Julian and Lawrence
90.8 × 47 cm, The Frick Collection, New York

52
GENTILE DA FABRIANO (*c.*1370–1427)
The Virgin and Child
110.4 × 66.3 cm, Museo Capitolare, Velletri

53
AMBROGIO LORENZETTI (active 1319–1348)
The Virgin and Child with Angels, SS. Dorothy,
Catherine of Alexandria and the Doctors of the Church
50.5 × 34.5 cm, Pinacoteca Nazionale, Siena

54
PIETRO LORENZETTI (active 1305–1348)
The Virgin and Child with Angels
145 × 122 cm, Galleria degli Uffizi, Florence

55
SIMONE MARTINI (*c*.1284–1344)
The Virgin and Child
67.5 × 48.3 cm, The Metropolitan Museum of Art,
New York: the Robert Lehman Collection

56
FRA ANGELICO (*c*.1395–1455)
The Virgin and Child with Angels
(central panel from a triptych)
260 × 330 cm, Museo di San Marco, Florence

57
FRA ANGELICO (*c*.1395–1455)
The Virgin and Child
100 × 60 cm, Galleria Sabauda, Turin

58
FILIPPO LIPPI (*c*.1406–1469)
The Adoration of the Child
129.5 × 118.5 cm, Gemäldegalerie Staatliche
Museen Preussischer Kulturbesitz, Berlin

59
FRANCESCO DI STEFANO PESELLINO
(c.1422–1457)
Virgin and Child with Six Saints
26.4 × 23.8 cm, The Metropolitan Museum of Art,
New York. Bequest of Mary Stillman Harkness

60
FRANCESCO DI STEFANO PESELLINO
(c.1422–1457)
*The Virgin and Child with the Young St John the Baptist
and Angels*
72.4 × 54 cm, The Toledo Museum of Art, Toledo
(Ohio). Gift of Edward Drummond Libbey

61
JAN VAN EYCK (active 1422–1441)
The Madonna at the Fountain
19 × 12.5 cm, Koninklijk Museum voor Schone
Kunsten, Antwerp

62
JAN VAN EYCK (active 1422–1441)
The Virgin in a Church
31 × 14 cm, Gemäldegalerie, Staatliche Museen
Preussischer Kulturbesitz, Berlin

63
FOLLOWER OF ROBERT CAMPIN (1370/9–1444)
The Virgin and Child with Saints in an Enclosed Garden
119.9 × 148.8 cm, National Gallery of Art,
Washington D.C.: the Samuel H. Kress
Collection

64
STEPHAN LOCHNER (active 1442–1451)
The Virgin and Child with Angels in the Rosegarden
51 × 40 cm, Wallraf-Richartz-Museum, Cologne

65
JAN VAN EYCK (active 1422—1441)
The Virgin and Child with Saints and a Donor
47.3 × 61.3 cm, The Frick Collection, New York

66
ROGIER VAN DER WEYDEN (*c.*1400—1464)
St Luke Painting the Virgin
135.3 × 108.8 cm, Museum of Fine Arts, Boston.
Gift of Mr & Mrs Henry Lee Higginson

67
ROGIER VAN DER WEYDEN (c.1400–1464)
The Virgin and Child
100 × 52 cm, Museo del Prado, Madrid

68
ROGIER VAN DER WEYDEN (c.1400–1464)
The Virgin and Child Standing in a Niche
18.5 × 12 cm, Kunsthistorisches Museum, Vienna

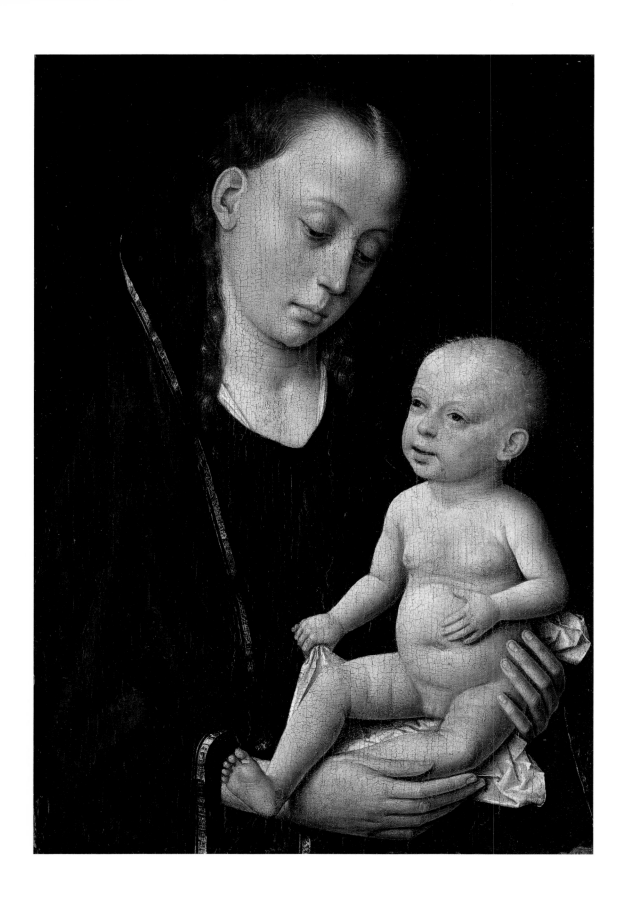

69
DIERIC BOUTS (active 1457, died 1475)
The Virgin and Child
23 × 15 cm, National Gallery of Art, Washington
D.C., Patron's Permanent Fund

70
WORKSHOP OF DIERIC BOUTS (1410/20–1475)
Virgin and Child
The Metropolitan Museum of Art, New York,
Jack and Belle Linsky Collection

71
MASTER OF THE ST LUCY LEGEND (active 1480)
The Virgin and Child with SS. Catherine of Alexandria,
Barbara, Ursula and Cecilia
79 × 60 cm, Detroit Institute of Arts

72
HANS MEMLINC (active c.1465–1494)
The Virgin and Child
37.5 × 28 cm, National Gallery, London

73
HANS MEMLINC (active *c*.1465–1494)
The Virgin and Child
44 × 33 cm, St John's Hospital, Bruges

74
GERARD DAVID (*c*.1460–1523)
The Virgin and Child
35 × 29 cm, Musées Royaux des Beaux-Arts,
Brussels

75
GIOVANNI BELLINI (c.1430–1516)
The Virgin and Child 52 × 42.5 cm, Museo Correr
e Quadreria Correr, Venice

76
SANDRO BOTTICELLI (1445–1510)
The Virgin and Child 91 × 73 cm, Städelsches
Kunstinstitut und Städtische Galerie, Frankfurt

78

ANDREA MANTEGNA (1430/1–1506)
The Virgin and Child
43 × 32 cm, Gemäldegalerie Staatliche Museen
Preussischer Kulturbesitz, Berlin

77

GIOVANNI BELLINI (c.1430–1516)
The Virgin and Child with a Greek Inscription
82 × 62 cm, Pinacoteca di Brera, Milan

79
HANS MEMLINC (active *c*.1465–1494)
The Virgin and Child
24.8 cm (diameter), The Metropolitan Museum of
Art, New York: the Friedsam Collection

80
HANS MEMLINC (active 1465–1494)
*The Virgin and Child Enthroned with an Angel and a
Donor*
69 × 74 cm, Kunsthistorisches Museum, Vienna

81

CARLO CRIVELLI (1430/5–c.1500)
The Virgin and Child (Madonna della Candeletta)
218 × 75 cm, Pinacoteca di Brera, Milan

82

PIERO DELLA FRANCESCA (c.1416–1492)
Madonna della Misericordia
273 × 323 cm, Pinacoteca Comunale Borgo
Sansepolcro

83
ANDREA MANTEGNA (1430/1–1506)
The Virgin and Child
43 × 45 cm, Museo Poldi-Pezzoli, Milan

84
MASTER OF THE MAGDALEN LEGEND
(c.1483–1527)
The Virgin and Child
26.5 × 18.4 cm, Musées Royaux des Beaux-Arts,
Brussels

85
SANDRO BOTTICELLI (1445–1510)
The Madonna of the Magnificat
118 cm (diameter), Galleria degli Uffizi, Florence

86
SANDRO BOTTICELLI (1445–1510)
The Virgin and Child with a Book
58 × 39.5 cm, Museo Poldi-Pezzoli, Milan

IOANNES BELLINVS

87
GIOVANNI BELLINI (c.1430—1516)
The Virgin and Child
88.9 × 71.1 cm, The Metropolitan Museum of Art,
New York. The Rogers Fund

88
GIOVANNI BELLINI (c.1430—1516)
The Madonna of the Pear
83 × 66 cm, Gallerie dell' Accademia Carrara,
Bergamo

IOANNES BELLINVS
P

89
ATTRIBUTED TO TITIAN (TIZIANO VECELLIO)
(c.1477–1576)
Virgin and Child with SS. Anthony of Padua and Roch
92 × 133 cm, Museo del Prado, Madrid

90
TITIAN (TIZIANO VECELLIO) (c.1477–1576)
The Virgin and Child (The Gipsy Madonna)
65.8 × 83.5 cm, Kunsthistorisches Museum, Vienna

91 ·
ANONYMOUS, FERRARESE SCHOOL
The Virgin and Child with two Angels
58.5 × 44 cm, National Gallery of Scotland,
Edinburgh

92
VITTORE CARPACCIO (*c*.1460–1523/6)
The Virgin and Child Enthroned with Angels
138 × 171 cm, Scuola di San Giorgio degli
Schiavoni, Venice

93
ALBRECHT DÜRER (1471–1528)
The Virgin and Child
24 × 18 cm, Kunsthistorisches Museum, Vienna

94
GIOVANNI BELLINI (c.1430–1516)
The Madonna of the Meadow
67 × 86 cm, National Gallery, London

95
NICHOLAS FROMENT
(active 1461–1483)
The Virgin in the Burning Bush
410 × 305 cm, Saint Sauveur
Cathedral, Aix-en-Provence

96
GIORGIONE (GIORGIO BARBARELLI)
(*c.*1478–1510)
The Virgin and Child Enthroned
200 × 152 cm, Veneto Duomo,
Castelfranco

97
GIOVANNI BELLINI (*c.*1430–1516) *The Virgin and Child Enthroned* 500 × 235 cm, San Zaccaria, Venice

98
TITIAN (TIZIANO VECELLIO) (c.1477–1576)
The Virgin and Child (The Madonna of the Cherries)
81 × 99.5 cm, Kunsthistorisches Museum, Vienna

99
SEBASTIANO DEL PIOMBO (*c*.1485–1547)
The Holy Family with St John the Baptist and a Donor
97.8 × 106.7 cm, National Gallery, London

100
LEONARDO DA VINCI (1452–1519)
The Madonna with the Carnation
62 × 47.5 cm, Alte Pinakothek, Munich

101
ANDREA VERROCCHIO (*c.*1435–1488)
The Virgin and Child
75.5 × 54.8 cm, Gemäldegalerie Staatliche Museen
Preussischer Kulturbesitz, Berlin

102
DOMENICO GHIRLANDAIO (1449–1494)
The Virgin and Child
73.4 × 50.8 cm, National Gallery of Art,
Washington D.C.: the Samuel H. Kress Collection

103
PIETRO PERUGINO (*c.*1445–1523)
The Virgin and Child
70.2 × 50.8 cm, National Gallery of Art,
Washington D.C.: the Samuel H. Kress Collection

104
RAPHAEL (RAFFAELLO SANZIO) (1483–1520)
The Virgin and Child with the Young St John the Baptist
and another Child (The Terranuova Madonna)
86 cm (diameter), Gemäldegalerie Staatliche
Museen Preussischer Kulturbesitz, Berlin

105
RAPHAEL (RAFFAELLO SANZIO) (1483–1520)
The Virgin and Child (The Large Cowper Madonna)
80.7 × 57.5 cm, National Gallery of Art,
Washington D.C.; the Andrew W. Mellon
Collection

106
FRANCESCO FRANCIA (active 1482–1517)
The Virgin and Child
61 × 46 cm, The Metropolitan Museum of Art,
New York. Gift of Lewis C. Ledyard III,
Mrs Victor Onet and Mrs T. F. Turner,
in memory of Lewis C. Ledyard

107
FRANCIABIGIO (FRANCESCO DI CRISTOFANO)
(*c.*1482–1525) *The Virgin and Child*
90 × 70 cm, Pinacoteca Nazionale, Bologna

108
LUCAS CRANACH THE ELDER (1472–1553)
The Virgin and Child
71.1 × 52.1 cm, National Gallery of Art,
Washington D.C. Gift of Adolf Caspar Miller

109
HANS BALDUNG GRIEN (1484/5–1545)
The Virgin and Child with an Angel
91 × 64 cm, Gemäldegalerie Staatliche Museen
Preussischer Kulturbesitz, Berlin

110

GERARD DAVID (*c.*1460–1523)
Virgin and Child with Angels
Metropolitan Museum of Art, New York
Gift of Mr and Mrs Charles Wrightsman

111

BERNAERT VAN ORLEY (*c.*1492–1541/2)
The Virgin and Child with Angels
by a Fountain 85.4 × 69.9 cm,
The Metropolitan Museum of Art, New York
Bequest of Benjamin Altman

112
ANDREA DEL SARTO (1486–1530)
The Madonna of the Harpies
208 × 178 cm, Galleria degli Uffizi, Florence

113
BUGIARDINI (1475–1554)
The Virgin and Child with SS. Mary Magdalen and John the Baptist
194.3 × 165.6 cm, The Metropolitan Museum of Art, New York. Fletcher Fund

114
ANDREA DEL SARTO (1486–1530)
Head of the Madonna (fragment)
38.1 × 29.2 cm, The Metropolitan Museum of Art,
New York. Bequest of Michael Friedsam: the
Friedsam Collection

115
ANTONIO ALLEGRI CORREGGIO (c.1494–1534)
The Virgin and Child with the Young St John the Baptist
64.2 × 50.4 cm, The Art Institute of Chicago.
Clyde M. Carr Fund

116

ANTONIO ALLEGRI CORREGGIO (*c*.1494–1534)
The Madonna of the Basket
33 × 25 cm, National Gallery, London

117
AGNOLO BRONZINO (1503–1572)
The Holy Family with St Anne and the young St John the Baptist
124.5 × 99.5 cm, Kunsthistorisches Museum, Vienna

118
JAN GOSSAERT (1475/8–1532)
The Virgin and Child
Koninklijk Museum voor Schone Kunsten, Antwerp

119
HANS HOLBEIN THE YOUNGER (1496/7–1543)
The Virgin and Child with Members of the Meyer Family
146.5 × 102 cm, Schlossmuseum, Darmstadt

120
JAN GOSSAERT (1475/8–1532)
The Virgin and Child
47.7 × 38.2 cm, Gemäldegalerie Staatliche Museen
Preussischer Kulturbesitz, Berlin

121
JOOS VAN CLEVE (c.1464–1540)
The Virgin and Child
73.5 × 54.5 cm, The Metropolitan Museum of Art,
New York: the Jack and Belle Linsky Collection

122
QUINTEN MASSYS (1465/6–1530)
The Virgin Standing with Angels
54.5 × 37.5 cm, Musée des Beaux-Arts, Lyons

123
QUINTEN MASSYS (1465/6–1530)
The Virgin and Child Enthroned
130 × 86 cm, Musée Royaux des Beaux-Arts,
Brussels

124
PAOLO VERONESE (1528–1588)
The Virgin and Child with the Young St John the
Baptist, SS. Elizabeth and Catherine of Alexandria
102.9 × 156.8 cm, The Putnam Foundation
Timken Art Gallery, San Diego, California

125
TITIAN (TIZIANO VECELLIO) (c.1477–1576)
The Virgin and Child
75.6 × 63.2 cm, National Gallery, London

126
DOMENICO TINTORETTO (*c*.1560–1635)
The Madonna of the Stars
92.7 × 72.7 cm, National Gallery of Art,
Washington D.C.: the Ralph and Mary Booth
Collection

127
EL GRECO (DOMENIKOS THEOTOCOPOULOS)
(1541–1614)
The Holy Family with St Anne (detail)
138 × 103.5 cm, Svepmúvészeti Museum (Museum
of Fine Arts), Budapest

128
AGOSTINO CARRACCI (1557–1602)
The Virgin and Child with the Young St John the Baptist
and SS. Nicholas, Cecilia and Margaret
153 × 120 cm, Galleria Nazionale di Parma

129
ANTHONY VAN DYCK (1599–1641)
The Virgin and Child
64.1 × 49.5 cm, The Metropolitan Museum of Art,
New York. Fletcher Fund

130

ANTHONY VAN DYCK (1599–1641)
The Virgin and Child with St Catherine of Alexandria
109.2 × 90.8 cm, The Metropolitan Museum of Art,
New York. Bequest of Lilian S. Timken

131

JUSEPE DE RIBERA (1591–1652)
*The Holy Family with SS. Anne and Catherine of
Alexandria*
209.6 × 154.3 cm, The Metropolitan Museum of
Art, New York. Samuel D. Lee Fund

132
MICHELANGELO MERISI DA CARAVAGGIO
(1571–1610)
The Madonna of Loreto
260 × 150 cm, San Agostino, Rome

133
LAVINIA FONTANA (1552–1614)
The Virgin Adoring the Sleeping Child
Museum of Fine Arts, Boston

134
DOMENICO FETTI (*c.*1589–1623)
*The Virgin and Child with SS. Catherine of Alexandria,
Peter Martyr and Dominic (The Mystic Marriage of St
Catherine)*
229.5 × 140.5 cm, Kunsthistorisches Museum,
Vienna

135
BARTOLOMÉ ESTEBAN MURILLO (1617/18–1682)
The Virgin and Child
165.7 × 109.2 cm, The Metropolitan Museum of
Art, New York. Rogers Fund

136
GIOVANNI BATTISTA TIEPOLO (1696–1770)
The Madonna of the Goldfinch
63.2 × 50.2 cm, National Gallery of Art,
Washington D.C.: the Samuel H. Kress
Collection

The Deposition & Pietà

137
SIMONE MARTINI (c.1284–1344)
The Entombment
23.7 × 16.7 cm, Gemäldegalerie Staatliche Museen
Preussischer Kulturbesitz, Berlin

138
DUCCIO DI BUONINSEGNA (active 1278–1318/9)
The Deposition from the Cross
50 × 53.7 cm, Museo dell' Opera della
Metropolitana, Siena

139
ROGIER VAN DER WEYDEN (1399/1400–1464)
The Deposition from the Cross
220 × 262 cm, Museo del Prado, Madrid

140
COLYN DE COTER (*c.*1455–1538/9)
The Deposition from the Cross
109 × 83.5 cm, Staatsgalerie, Stuttgart

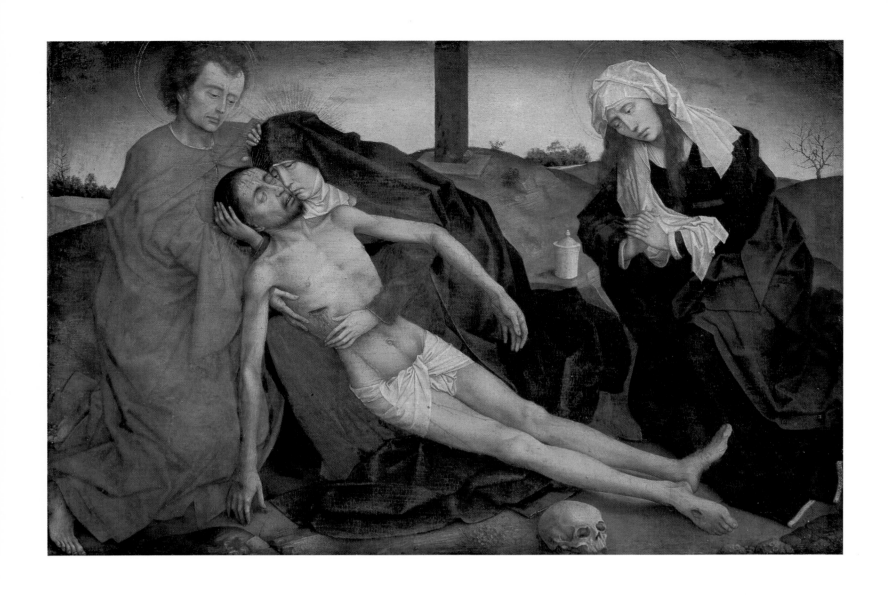

141
ROGIER VAN DER WEYDEN (c.1400–1464)
The Pietà
32.2 × 47.2 cm, Musées Royaux des Beaux-Arts,
Brussels

142
GERARD DAVID (active c.1484–1523)
The Pietà
80 × 50 cm, Oskar Reinhart Collection, Winterthur

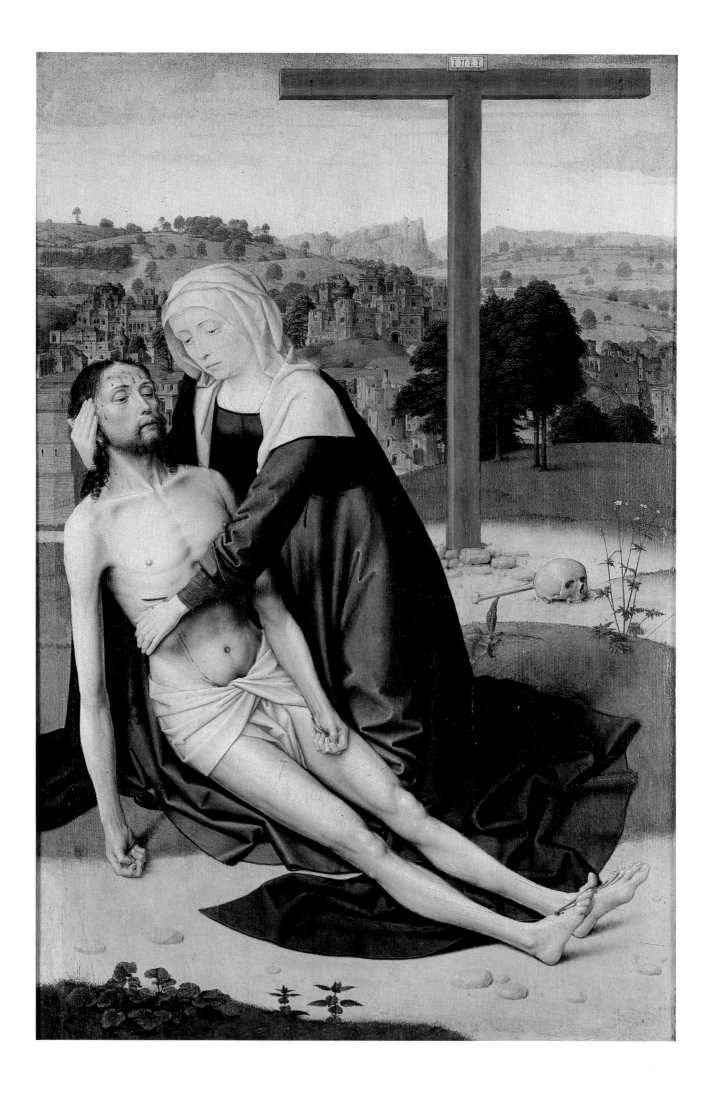

143
ATTRIBUTED TO ENGUERRAND QUARTON
(active 1444–1466)
The Pietà
163 × 218.5 cm, Musée du Louvre, Paris

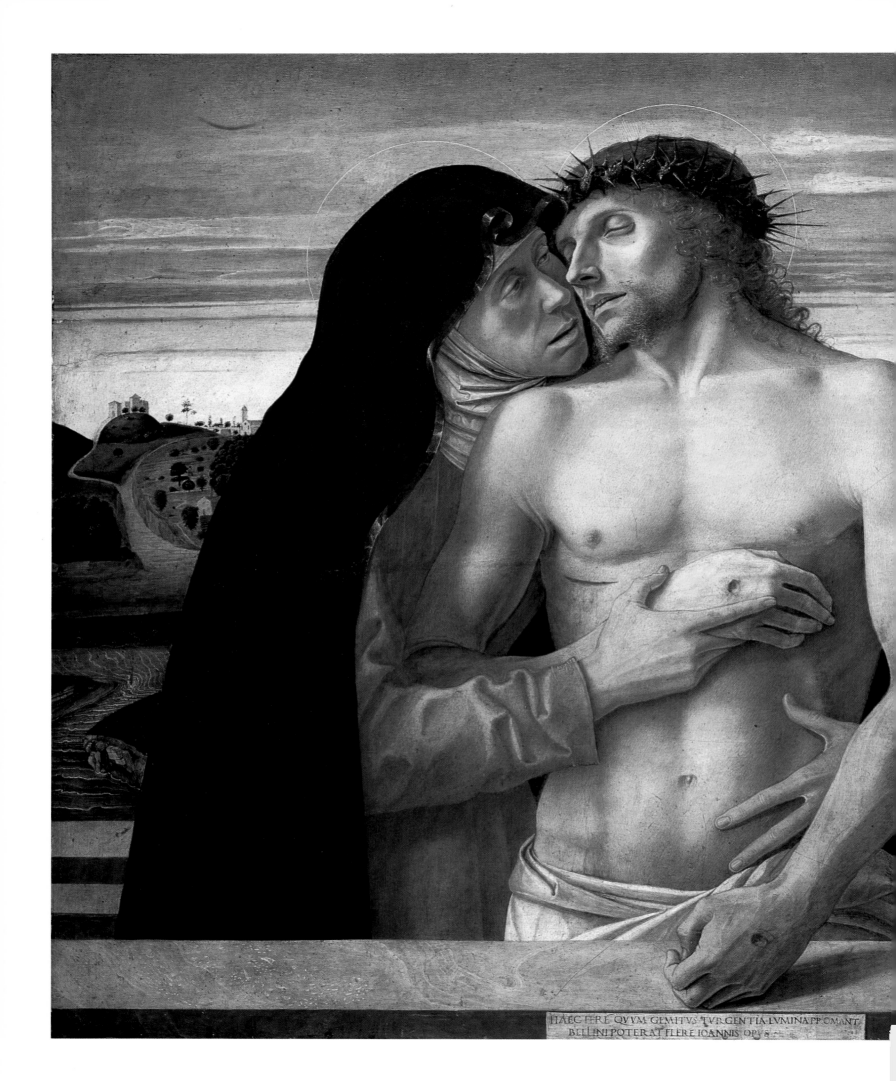

HAEC FERE QVVM GEMITVS TVRGENTIA LVMINA PROMANT
BELLINI POTERAT FLERE IOANNIS OPVS

144
GIOVANNI BELLINI (c.1430–1516)
The Pietà
87 × 107 cm, Pinacoteca di Brera, Milan

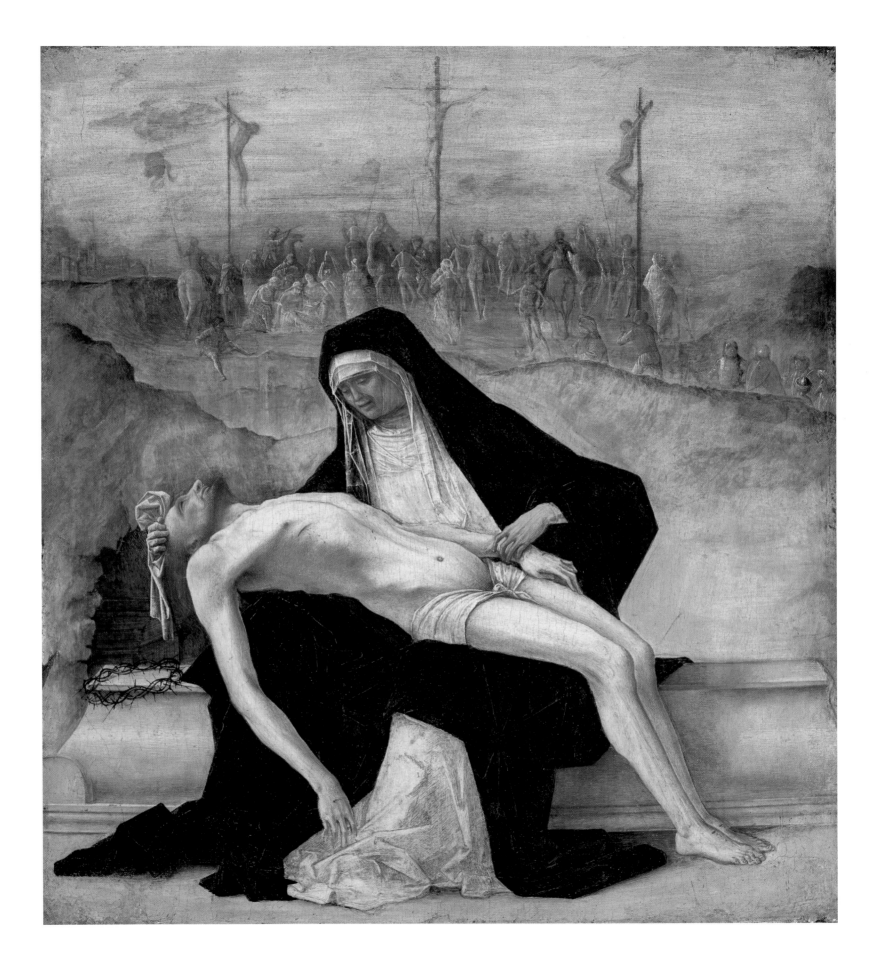

145
DIERIC BOUTS (active 1457, died 1475)
Mater Dolorosa
37 × 28 cm, The Art Institute of Chicago.
Chester D. Tripp Endowment Fund

146
ERCOLE DE' ROBERTI (active 1479–1496)
The Pietà
34.3 × 31.3 cm, Walker Art Gallery, Liverpool

147
SANDRO BOTTICELLI (1445–1510)
The Pietà
110 × 207 cm, Alte Pinakothek, Munich

148
SANDRO BOTTICELLI (1445–1510)
The Pietà
107 × 71 cm, Museo Poldi-Pezzoli, Milan

149
TITIAN (TIZIANO VECELLIO) (c.1477–1576)
The Pietà
353 × 348 cm, Galleria dell' Accademia, Venice

150
ANNIBALE CARRACCI (1560–1609)
The Pietà
156 × 149 cm, Museo e Gallerie di Capodimonte,
Naples

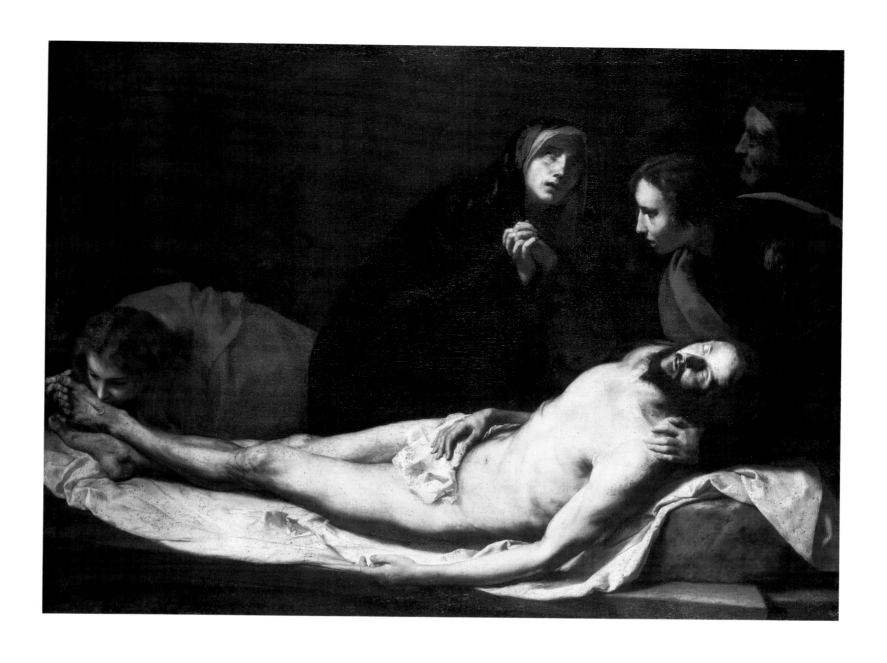

151
JUSEPE DE RIBERA (1591–1652)
The Pietà
157 × 210 cm, Thyssen-Bornemisza Collection,
Lugano

The Death, Assumption
& Coronation of the Virgin

152
DUCCIO DI BUONINSEGNA (active 1278–1318/19)
The Funeral of the Virgin
58 × 52.5 cm, Museo dell' Opera del Duomo, Siena

153
DUCCIO DI BUONINSEGNA (active 1278–1318/19)
The Apostles' Farewell to the Virgin
41.5 × 54 cm, Museo dell' Opera della
Metropolitana, Siena

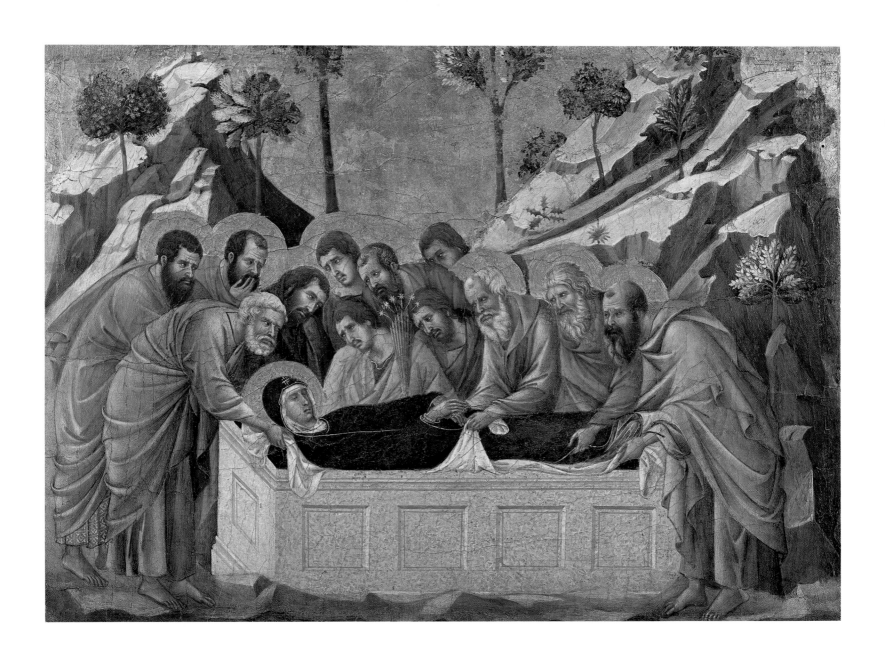

154
DUCCIO DI BUONINSEGNA (active 1278–1318/19)
The Burial of the Virgin
41.2 × 54 cm, Museo dell' Opera della
Metropolitana, Siena

155
PIETER BRUEGEL THE ELDER
(c.1525/30–1569)
The Death of the Virgin
36 × 54.5 cm, Upton House, Banbury

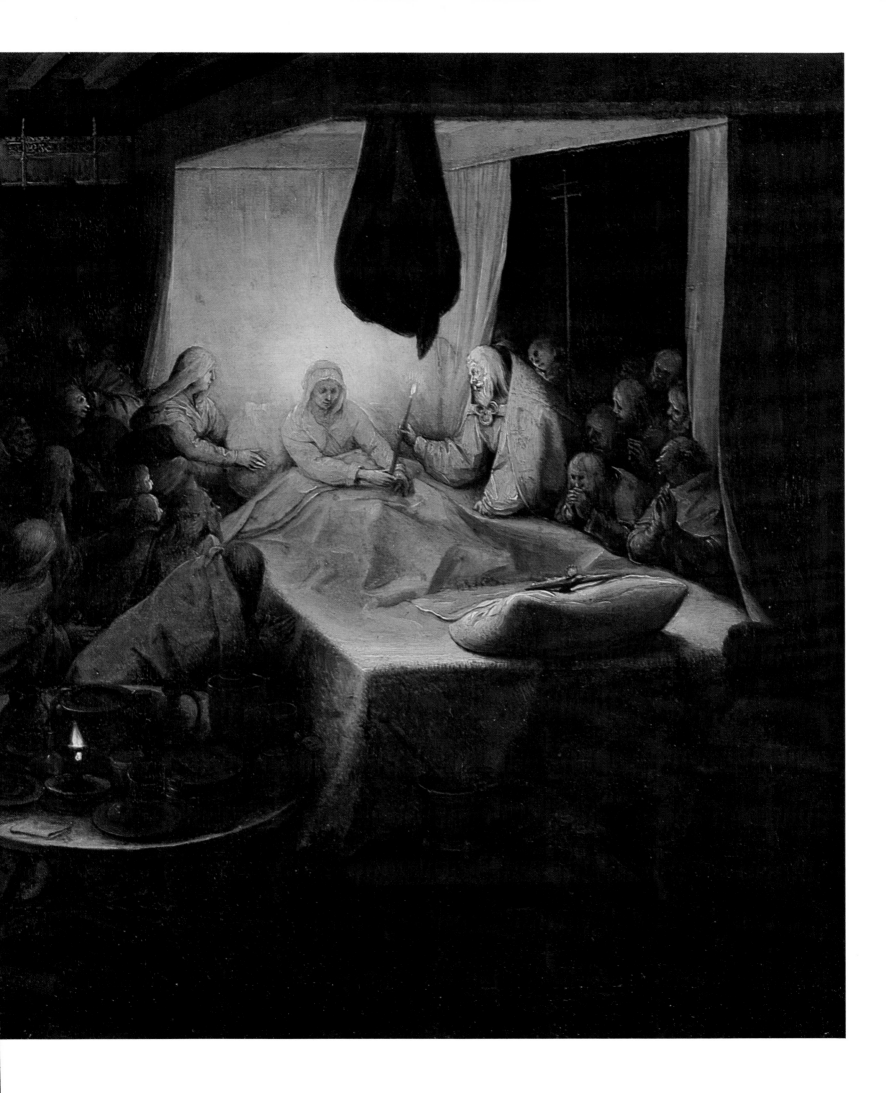

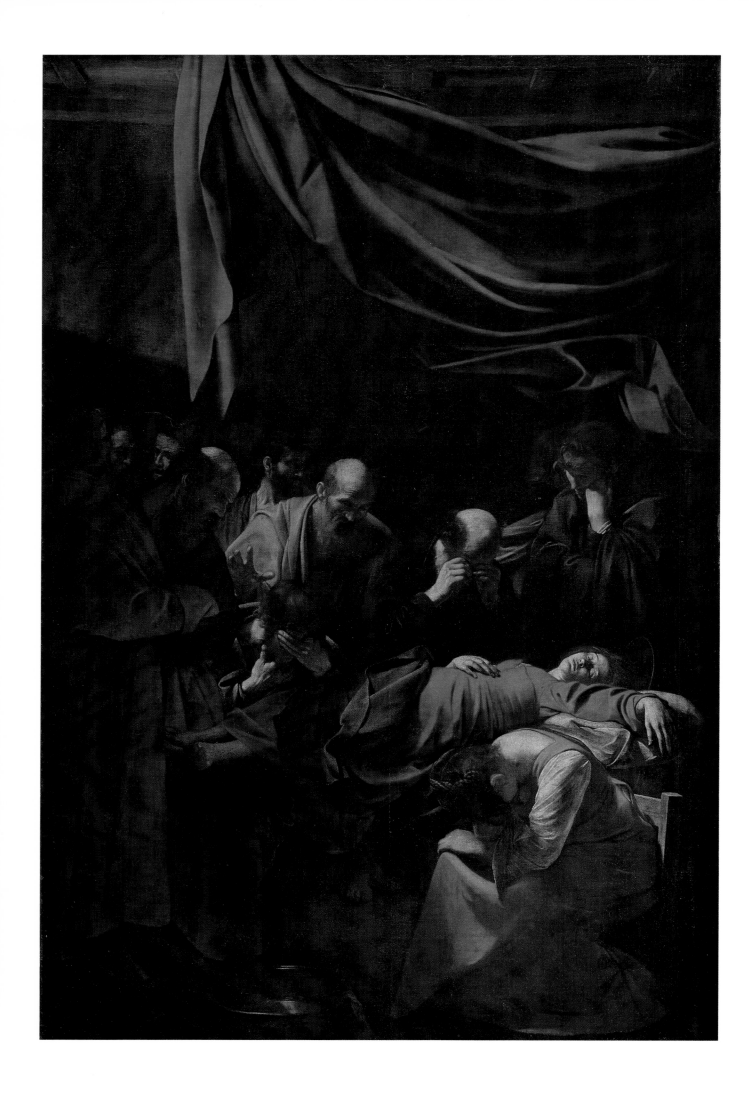

156
MICHELANGELO MERISI DA CARAVAGGIO
(1571–1610)
The Death of the Virgin
369 × 245 cm, Musée du Louvre, Paris

157
ANDREA DEL CASTAGNO (1417/19–1457)
The Assumption of the Virgin with SS. Julian and Miniatus
131 × 150.5 cm, Gemäldegalerie Staatliche Museen
Preussischer Kulturbesitz, Berlin

158
TITIAN (TIZIANO VECELLIO) (*c*.1477–1576)
The Assumption of the Virgin
690 × 360 cm, Santa Maria dei Frari, Venice

159
EL GRECO (DOMENIKOS THEOTOCOPOULOS)
(1541–1614)
The Assumption of the Virgin
301.3 × 228.7 cm, The Art Institute of Chicago,
Gift of Nancy Atwood Sprague in memory of
Albert Arnold Sprague

160

PAOLO and GIOVANNI VENEZIANO (active
1321–1358)
The Coronation of the Virgin
110 × 68.5 cm, The Frick Collection, New York

161

MARIOTTO DI NARDO (recorded 1394–1431)
The Coronation of the Virgin
131.7 × 68.5 cm, The Minneapolis Institute of Arts

162

GENTILE DA FABRIANO (c.1370–1427)
The Coronation of the Virgin
158 × 79 cm, Pinacoteca di Brera, Milan

163
FRA ANGELICO (*c.*1395–1455)
The Coronation of the Virgin
209 × 206 cm, Musée du Louvre, Paris

164
GIOVANNI BELLINI (c.1430–1516)
The Coronation of the Virgin
262 × 240 cm, Museo Civico, Pesaro

165
DIEGO VELÁZQUEZ (1599–1660)
The Coronation of the Virgin by the Trinity
176 × 124 cm, Museo del Prado, Madrid

Notes on the Plates

The task of the religious artist is to translate articles of faith into visual images that are at once immediately comprehensible and aesthetically pleasing to the beholder. The early Christians in the catacombs of imperial Rome produced images that helped to identify a burgeoning religion and to codify new principles of faith in the face of state repression. At this primitive stage of development of Christianity, symbols — the fish, the cross — served as the primary images, but these were soon supplemented by attempts at simple narrative illustrating the most dramatic moments of the life of Christ. From its origins as a cult Christianity grew in power and influence within the Roman Empire and became its official religion. Imperial iconography, which glorified the Roman Emperors in various heroic and divine roles, was adapted to suit the new religious context, a transformation which took place with surprising ease, so that the narrative elements expanded rapidly.

Following the decline of the Western Roman Empire in the fourth century, a new Christian metropolis was established in the East, at Byzantium (Constantinople). Here the much respected tradition of classical art mingled with the vitality of oriental art, so that it was in the eastern Mediterranean that Christian art then entered a critical stage of its development. At first the Byzantine style was stiff and hieratic in accordance with the nature of the subject-matter. Images of God the Father, the Virgin Mary or Christ in Majesty were formal and restrained. Some — those decorating the apse of a church, for example — were on a colossal scale and were intended to be awe-inspiring. Reverence tinged with fear was the emotion kindled by such images, but works on a smaller scale, such as painted icons, had a different effect. Certainly by the sixth century icons, particularly those displayed in the private sphere, were seen as objects offering divine protection and assistance. Such works of art were gradually given a status of their own in the divine order of the universe. An icon became an agent through which the believer could communicate directly with the sacred figure delineated, and ultimately came to be venerated as a surrogate for that figure. This development in turn led in the eighth century to a reaction known as Iconoclasm; its leading figures criticized the veneration of icons as a form of idolatry, and tried to redefine the role of images in imperial and religious art. As a result of such controversies, Byzantine art developed a firm iconographical basis for Christian art both in terms of standardized images of Christ and the Virgin, and the narrative accounts illustrating scriptural scenes. The representation of the Virgin and Child, for example, could be carried out in a number of ways: these included the Madonna enthroned with the Child, the Madonna presenting the Child to the people, the Child caressing the Madonna's cheek, the Madonna indicating the Child as the Way of Truth, and the Madonna feeding the Child.

From the eleventh century onwards later Byzantine art proved to be an important inspirational force in the revival of the arts in the West, particularly in Italy. Byzantine art was seen to be the repository of classical tradition and the codifier of Christian iconography. Thirteenth- and fourteenth-century Italian art was strongly influenced by Byzantine images and works of art in various forms. There are parallels for the paintings of Giotto and Duccio in Byzantine art but it is in such works as the frescoes by Giotto in the Arena Chapel or the narrative scenes on Duccio's Maestà that the first stirrings of Renaissance art can be seen. Convincingly drawn people set within recognizable surroundings resulted in works that the viewer could identify with easily as part of his or her own world. Yet the continuing development of art in the West was not due solely to the reimportation of stylistic and iconographic features from the east: it was also due in large part to the use of new literary sources that gave artists fresh inspiration. Beyond the Bible there was throughout the Middle Ages a growing amount of exegetical literature mainly in the form of commentaries to sacred texts. In addition, however, there were such texts as *The Golden Legend* of Jacobus de Voragine (*c*.1230–*c*.1298), Archbishop of Genoa, which was essentially a hagiographical work recounting incidents or anecdotes from the lives of the saints, and including treatises on the main Christian festivals. A source popular during the fourteenth century was the *Meditations on the Life of Christ* which offered an extempore account of the life of Christ that was primarily used for the edification of monastic communities at mealtimes, where it was read aloud. The *Meditations* are written in an intensely emotional vein imploring the reader or listener to empathize with the incidents in the narrative, and, even if not consulted directly by artists, it is the tone of this account of Christ's life that is important. With the growth of monasteries and the advent of mysticism new themes could be developed or introduced into art — the Madonna della Misericordia, the Madonna of the Rosegarden, the Seven Joys and Seven Sorrows of the Virgin, the Immaculate Conception, and the

Madonna dell' Umiltà. Not surprisingly, by the fifteenth century certain theologians in Italy were protesting at the freedom with which artists were interpreting more traditional religious themes. The Archbishop of Florence, Antonio Pierozzi (later St Antonio) (1389–1459) in his *Summa Theologica* argued that painters 'are to be reprimanded when they paint things contrary to the faith, when they make an image of the Trinity as one person with three heads, which is monstrous in the nature of things, or, in the Annunciation of the Virgin, a formed little child, that is Jesus, being sent into the womb of the Virgin, as if his body were not derived from the substance of the Virgin, or the little Jesus with a tablet of letters, whereas he did not learn from man. Nor are they to be praised who paint apocryphal tales, such as midwives in the Nativity, or the Virgin's girdle thrown down to Thomas the Apostle during Assumption because of his doubt, and the like. To paint curiosities in stories of the saints or in churches, which have no value in stimulating devotion, but laughter and vanity, such as monkeys, or dogs chasing hares, or the like, or vain adornments of clothing, appears superfluous and vain.' Such strictures might seem to have limited artists, but, given the narrow range and focus of subject-matter, it is amazing what variety there is in any series of images of the Virgin extending down the centuries and thus proving the continuing potency of the theme.

With the arrival of the Renaissance, however, it became axiomatic for painters to treat the divine as an extension of the real world. Symptomatic of this was the development of the *sacra conversazione* altarpiece in which saints and even donors inhabited the same space and enacted a dialogue with the sacred figures. The rediscovery of the classical past by the humanists encouraged the secularization of art so that painters were as much concerned with mythological subjects as religious ones. Indeed, these two worlds often overlapped in the sphere of iconography or philosophy where, for example, neoplatonism amounted to a reinterpretation of Christianity. In Northern Europe the Reformation purged religion of many of its impurities, while perhaps taking on others. Images of the Virgin and Child by Netherlandish and German artists of the late fifteenth century have a degree of informality and accessibility that Italian artists rarely attempted. The theme of the Holy Family was often embellished with charming domestic anecdote. By contrast, the classicizing principles of the High Renaissance led to a

search for purity of form that could be equated with the ideal and so was admirably suited to religious art.

The altarpieces and series of Madonnas by Raphael mark the apogee of this moment in the history of art. The reaction against the High Renaissance, during the middle decades of the sixteenth century, occurs with Mannerism where elegant style tended to dominate subject-matter. Mannerism in turn helped to initiate the Baroque style, characterized by twisted forms spiralling upwards within extravagantly illusionistic settings. For many the Baroque, as in the church of the Gesù in Rome decorated by Gaulli, is the quintessential expression of the religious in art, though for others it marks the evaporation of fine feeling and conviction in overblown and essentially superficial images of ecstasy.

Such striving for effect complements the theoretical concepts of the Counter-Reformation of the mid-seventeenth century, which artists like Velázquez and Murillo so splendidly uphold. By the eighteenth century, however, religious art was again threatened, this time by the growth of the Enlightenment. While much of the manual dexterity and visual pyrotechnics remained, the degree of commitment was considerably less. Even though artists such as G. B. Tiepolo were capable of devising wholly original religious iconography, his treatment of the Virgin gives us none of the moral security that we derive from earlier works. Renaissance painters such as Fra Angelico, Piero della Francesca and Giovanni Bellini addressed themselves wholeheartedly to the traditional qualities of the Virgin's character and, by doing so, sustained her through their own works as a sacred and timeless being.

Christopher Lloyd

Notes on the Plates

The Icon & the Byzantine Tradition

1

RUSSIAN SCHOOL (twelfth century)
The Virgin of the Great Panagia
(called *The Virgin Orant of Yaroslavl*)
192 × 122 cm, Tretyakov Gallery, Moscow

This icon was discovered in 1919 in the Convent of the Transfiguration at Yaroslavl, but it may not originally have come from there and some scholars have suggested Kiev or Vladimir as alternative locations. The Virgin stands staring directly at the viewer with her arms extended outwards in the gesture denoting prayer. The majestic figure dressed in dark blue drapery with gold highlights is silhouetted against the gold background. The flesh tones are warm, and different hues of red are used for Christ's overmantle and the cushion at the Virgin's feet. The mantle hanging from the Virgin's shoulders gives the figure a powerful presence, and the white halo seems to push her forwards. The quality of the icon is such that the monumentality of the Virgin does not induce fear in the beholder; rather, the simple form and calm gesture evoke feelings of affection and admiration. The Christ Child is shown symbolically in a circle: it is as though by extending her arms the Virgin reveals the Child to the world and bids us worship Him.

2

MASTER OF SS. COSMAS AND DAMIAN
(Pisan school, 1265–1285)
The Virgin and Child
64 × 44 cm, Fogg Art Museum,
Harvard University, Cambridge (Mass.).
Friends of the Fogg Art Museum Fund

The panel shows the influence of Byzantine art on Italian painting. Owing to its trading connections, Pisa was in close contact with Constantinople during the thirteenth century. The Master of SS. Cosmas and Damian was a follower of Giunta Pisano, but he was also subject to the influence of the Florentine, Coppo di Marcovaldo. During the mid-thirteenth century the Pisan school was in the vanguard of Italian painting, mainly as a result of Giunto Pisano's contribution most evident today in his three dramatic Crucifixes (Assisi, Bologna, Pisa). Not many works attributable to the Master of SS. Cosmas and Damian are known, and those that do survive are all depictions of *The Virgin and Child*. The stylistic features of thirteenth-century panel painting are fully revealed in this example. The earthy colours offset by the Virgin's kerchief, the clear outlines, the heavy mark of shadow defining the jaw, the almond-shaped eyes with the arched eyebrows, and the small mouths are the hallmarks of late thirteenth-century Pisan painting. This powerful image can be described as primitive, but that should not be taken to mean that the style lacks skill: the drawing of the eyes, the handling of the draperies and the laying in of flesh tones on the cheeks are technically very assured.

3

EL GRECO (DOMENIKOS THEOTOKOPOULOS)
(1541–1614)
St Luke Painting the Virgin and Child
42 × 33 cm, Benaki Museum, Athens

El Greco was born on the Greek island of Crete (at that time under Venetian rule), where he is documented in 1562. His first paintings were icons some of which are signed in Greek with his full name, Domenikos Theotokopoulos. St Luke himself was by origin also a Greek: a physician, he was a disciple of St Paul whom he accompanied on some of his missionary journeys. The gospel written by St Luke is one of the main sources for the early life of Christ, but it is also notable for its compassion in the recounting of parables and of Christ's death. As early as the eighth century in the eastern Mediterranean legend proclaimed that St Luke was also a painter who, it was traditionally believed, painted the Virgin. In time this became a popular subject for painters, particularly in the Netherlands, and such pictures today provide valuable information about the materials and insight into the practices of contemporary artists. This icon is badly damaged — the figure of St Luke almost completely obliterated — but the eye readily focuses on the small panel depicting the Virgin and Child on the easel. El Greco's style was to be dramatically transformed when he left Crete for an extended visit to the Italian mainland c.1565, working in Venice and Rome.

The Apocryphal Life of the Virgin

4

DIEGO VELÁZQUEZ (1599–1660)
The Virgin of the Immaculate Conception
134.6 × 101.6 cm, National Gallery, London

The painting is one of Velázquez's earliest works; it most probably formed a pendant to *St John the Evangelist on the Island of Patmos* (also in the National Gallery, London). Both were executed (c.1618) for the Convent of Shod Carmelites in Seville. Velázquez rapidly developed a naturalistic style which he also employed for his religious pictures. There is nothing idealized about this representation of the Virgin, even though she is portraying a difficult theological concept. Similarly, the realistic treatment of light helps, as in Caravaggio's paintings, to heighten the awareness of divine mystery. The influence of Velázquez's master and father-in-law, Francisco Pacheco, is still apparent in the composition and drawing of the Virgin, but the chiaroscuro effect of the white clouds set against a dark sky is exploited by the younger painter in a way that was beyond the capabilities of the older man. The theme of the Immaculate Conception is that the Virgin Mary was entirely free from the taint of Original Sin, so that she had been pure all her life when she gave birth to Christ. The term Immaculate Conception thus does not refer to the conception of Christ in the Virgin's womb, but to the Virgin's own conception in St Anne's womb. The validity of this doctrine had been much disputed since the Middle Ages, but artists began to depict it fairly regularly in Italy during the sixteenth century. During later centuries the doctrine became more widely accepted, although it was not ratified as an article of faith until as late as the mid-nineteenth

century. But in Spain, significantly, the doctrine received papal sanction in 1617 — just as Velázquez was preparing to paint this picture. 'In *The Immaculate Conception* the Virgin, serene and lofty in her purple-shadowed white gown and blue mantle, stands against the sun with the moon under her feet. Her face — framed by her golden-brown hair — and her hands are flawless, limpid shapes, loved as it were, by the smooth brushwork' (López-Rey). The landscape below, seen in penumbra, is filled with emblems from the Litany of the Virgin.

5

MAIR VON LANDSHUT (active c.1485–1510)
The Birth of the Virgin
38 × 31 cm, Gemäldegalerie Staatliche Museen Preussischer Kulturbesitz, Berlin

The artist was a painter, engraver and woodcut designer who was most probably born in Freising not far from Munich. He was active in Freising, Munich and Landshut. Both his paintings and his prints have a naïve charm that results in a highly personal rendering of traditional subject-matter. The *Birth of the Virgin*, which may originally have formed part of an altarpiece showing a full complement of scenes from the Life of the Virgin, is a fine example of Mair von Landshut's work. The architecture of the interior is somewhat whimsical and the figures are doll-like, with large heads balanced on thin necks. Indeed, the whole scene resembles a room in a doll's house with the angels playing at being mother in the lower left corner. Joachim and an angel attend to St Anne, while seen through the door is a servant preparing a meal. The strong colours are enhanced by the noctural effect of the lighting so that the whites appear particularly luminous. The coat-of-arms in the lower right corner is presumably a reference to the patron who commissioned the altarpiece to which this panel belonged. The curtain for enclosing the bed is drawn on the right, but on the left it has been gathered up like a sack. It is interesting to compare the purely descriptive use of this shape in the present painting with the dramatic effect it creates in Pieter Bruegel the Elder's *Death of the Virgin*. To a certain extent the composition, the vivid colouring, the unusual types and the eye for narrative incident are comparable with the style of Hans Holbein the Elder, whose major altarpiece of scenes from the Life of the Virgin in the cathedral at Augsburg dates from 1493.

6

GERARD DAVID (c.1460–1523)
Christ taking leave of his Mother
15.6 × 12.1 cm, The Metropolitan Museum of Art, New York. Bequest of Benjamin Altman

The panel is the right-hand wing of a diptych of which a *Virgin and Child with two Angels* (Upton House, National Trust) forms the left wing. David painted diptychs with these subjects several times. The composition of *Christ taking leave of his Mother* is skilfully composed to suit the curved top of the painting: the three-quarters length bodies bend towards one another echoing the shape of the arch. The Virgin is on the left of the group of female figures and it is to her that Christ speaks. The female attendant nearest to Christ sobs in contrast with the Virgin's more subdued pose. The narrative is reduced to a minimum and David concentrates on expression and gesture to generate emotion. As Friedlander wrote, 'His imagination is less preoccupied with what may actually have happened in a given time and place than with the meaning of the event in terms of Christian doctrine'. By treating the figures in close-up, David invests the picture with a hieratic significance. The source for the theme of Christ taking leave of his Mother is the fourteenth century manuscript *Meditations on the Life of Christ*, which recounts how Christ bade farewell to his mother at Bethany before entering Jerusalem for the last time. Although the text was well-known to Italian painters, this particular scene was more frequently painted by north European artists.

7
TITIAN (TIZIANO VECELLIO) (*c.*1477–1576)
The Presentation of the Virgin
335 × 775 cm, Galleria dell' Accademia, Venice

The painting is of unusually grand proportions, and is in fact still in its original position in the *albergo* of the Scuola di Santa Maria della Carità (now part of the Accademia). The work was painted between 1534 and 1538, and is one of the masterpieces of Venetian Renaissance painting. Titian was particularly skilful in creating a spacious setting closed in by buildings on the right and open on the left, where there is a view of distant mountains. The architecture has overtones of Rome — the pyramid of Caius Cestius is prominently quoted and various pieces of antique statuary are placed amidst the buildings. Yet Titian's main sources are really the architecture of Jacopo Sansovino and Sebastiano Serlio, whose designs would have been even closer to hand than those of ancient Rome. The subject of the painting could easily have been lost in such a setting, but the artist has cleverly exploited the possibilities of this situation. The diminutive form of the Virgin, for example — isolated from the other figures in the scene as she ascends the flight of steps — is an unforgettable image. Similarly, the old woman seated in the foreground with a basket of eggs and observing the event from behind the protection of the steps, acts as a link between the viewer and the main participants. Titian has included leading members of the Scuola della Carità in the group of supporting figures on the left. The painter's ability to integrate all the various elements of this large-scale composition into a single unit is testimony to his narrative powers.

The Annunciation

8
SIMONE MARTINI (*c.*1284–1344)
The Annunciation
184 × 114 cm (centre); 105 × 48 cm (each side panel), Galleria degli Uffizi, Florence

Although now in Florence, this panel was in fact painted as an altarpiece for Siena cathedral which housed a series of major altarpieces depicting incidents from the life of the Virgin commissioned from leading Sienese artists during the first half of the fourteenth century. The present picture is dated 1333 and was painted jointly with Lippo Memmi whose participation, however, was probably limited to the saints on either side. The painting is a spectacular

example of the Sienese school with its dependence on singing line and incandescent colour so suited to religious art. The figures are seen in silhouette against a gold background. The Virgin has been disturbed while reading, and turns almost languidly away from the Archangel Gabriel who carries an olive branch. The figures are placed far apart. Gabriel's wings extend upwards towards the apex of the arch on the left, while the Virgin is seated beneath the arch on the right. A vase of lilies marks the centre point immediately below God the Father. The void between the two principal figures is reduced by the greeting 'Hail Virgin Mary Full of Grace', which is incised into the gold ground and wafts across the empty space.

9
JAN VAN EYCK (active 1422–1441)
The Annunciation
each 39 × 24 cm, Thyssen-Bornemisza Collection, Lugano

The narrative is spread across two panels dating from the mid-1430s. Often such a feature would indicate that the paintings had once formed the folding wings of a triptych, but in fact there are no signs of hinges and no further images on the backs, which have been painted to simulate marble. It is likely, therefore, that van Eyck intended these two panels to be free-standing and so form a composition in their own right. The artist has adapted the technique known as grisaille, in which a monochrome white or off-white is applied against a dark background. The figures resemble pieces of sculpture in niches, and this imaginative effect is increased by the simulated mouldings of the frame. So faithful is van Eyck's rendering of reality that he shows the reflections of the two figures in the brightly polished black marble behind. As one scholar has written, it is difficult to tell where truth ends and fiction begins. In one sense van Eyck has readily and successfully exploited his technique for the purposes of creating a distinguished still-life painting, but he has also invested his figures with the actual qualities of sculpture. There is an emphasis on modelling and on corporeality, quite apart from the isolation of the figures that corresponds to how the Annunciation is shown in the sculptured groups of medieval cathedrals. Van Eyck's figures have a stillness and immobility that deliberately emulates such sculptured pairings.

10
FRA ANGELICO (*c.*1395–1455)
The Annunciation
194 × 194 cm, Museo del Prado, Madrid

The painting was originally an altarpiece in the monastic church of San Domenico, Fiesole, to which community the artist himself belonged for several years after joining the Dominican Order sometime between 1418 and 1420. The painting dates from the late 1440s. The scene takes place in a Renaissance *loggia*: the Virgin and the Archangel Gabriel are divided by a column, suggesting a distinction between the secular and the divine. The Virgin's pose is one of humility, anticipating the important role she is to play as mother of the Christ born to atone for the sins of mankind. The figures of Adam and Eve being expelled from the Garden of Eden in the left background are a direct reference to

the Fall of Man. The mystery of the incarnation is represented by the shaft of light issuing from heaven and directed diagonally towards the Virgin. God the Father is shown in the roundel above the central column of the *loggia*, symbolically presiding over the event. The predella of the altarpiece depicts other scenes from the life of the Virgin. The range of Fra Angelico's art is apparent in the precisely illuminated interior behind the main figures and the resplendent floral carpet indicating the Garden of Eden on the left.

11
ATTRIBUTED TO JAN VAN EYCK (active 1422–1441)
The Annunciation
77.5 × 64.5 cm, Metropolitan Museum of Art, New York. Bequest of Michael Friedsam, The Friedsam Collection

This representation of *The Annunciation* is unusual and is replete with symbolic overtones. The Archangel Gabriel confronts the Virgin standing at the entrance to a church. The façade of the church, however, is divided into two parts corresponding to different architectural styles. On the right is the plain Romanesque, with a single cylindrical shaft engaging a square pier. At the top of the shaft is a carved monkey, a symbol of evil normally equated with Eve and the Fall of Man. The Annunciation is the occasion for the declaration of Mary or the 'new' Eve, whose perfection is to overcome the sin of the 'old' Eve. Contrasting the Romanesque style of the right side of the façade is the Gothic architecture on the left, where the windows symbolize divine illumination and the white flowers purity. The decayed state of the wall and the worn appearance of the step at the entrance to the church suggest life under the 'old' law which is about to be replaced by the 'new' law represented by the building itself. Significantly, in the portal above the Virgin's head is an empty niche soon to be filled by a statue of the newborn Christ, who will be the keystone, both literally and metaphorically, of the 'new' dispensation. The close technique, microscopic attention to detail, and high finish allow the artist to enhance the composition with an abundance of learned references. Just as the eye is captivated by the visual content of the painting, so the mind is absorbed by the intellectual basis underlying the picture, which may have been painted during the 1420s.

12
PIERO DELLA FRANCESCA (*c.*1416–1492)
The Annunciation
329 × 193 cm, San Francesco, Arezzo

The fresco forms part of the extensive scheme decorating the choir of the church of San Francesco in Arezzo painted by Piero della Francesca during the 1450s and 1460s. The subject of the frescoes is the Legend of the True Cross, but the artist included this depiction of the Annunciation on the left-hand side of the altar wall. The protagonists are conceived on a monumental scale, and the composition as a whole has a gravity that can be associated with classical art. The Virgin is a poised and regal figure, and the Archangel Gabriel solemnly performs his duty watched over by the beneficent form of God the Father. The auspiciousness of the occasion is underscored by the richness of the architectural elements, such as the expertly proportioned column topped by an elegantly carved Corinthian capital and the broad entablature inlaid with differently coloured marbles. The figures are so economical in their movements that they seem almost to be part of the architecture. This sense of unity, derived in part from an underlying sense of geometry, is the essence of Piero della Francesca's art.

13
CARLO CRIVELLI (active 1457–1493)
The Annunciation with St Emidius
207 × 146.5 cm, National Gallery, London

This extravagantly decorative scene of the Annunciation was painted for the church of Santissima Annunziata in Ascoli. It is dated 1482 and was painted to commemorate the award in that year of certain political privileges to the town by Pope Sixtus IV. News of the event reached Ascoli on the feast of the Annunciation (25 March) which is presumably why this subject was chosen. The inscription along the lower edge refers to the papal privileges in question. A rare feature of the altarpiece is the ray representing the path of the Holy Ghost that pierces directly through the wall in a manner that resembles certain modern film techniques. It is also unusual for a saint to be present at the Annunciation. St Emidius, however, was the patron saint of Ascoli and he is shown holding a model of the town. He was obviously accorded a role in the scene in a burst of local patriotism. Crivelli provides the composition with a sumptuous setting: the lavishly carved pilasters, entablatures, arches and capitals, the mixture of brick and marble, and the comfortable interior of the Virgin's room, are set pieces. In the left half the artist has depicted a street scene with figures moving about the town and a little girl peering round a wall at the top of a flight of steps. The carpets and potted plants are a typically Venetian touch used by other artists such as Antonello de Messina. Some of these details, for example the peacock, are symbolic, but others are purely anecdotal.

14
SANDRO BOTTICELLI (1445–1510)
The Annunciation
150 × 156 cm, Galleria degli Uffizi, Florence

The painting was executed in 1489/90 as an altarpiece for a chapel within the church of Santa Maria Maddalena de' Pazzi, Florence. It is on a fairly large scale and there is a feeling of spaciousness in the sparse furnishing of the room and the view through to the placid landscape. The view reveals a certain kinship with Flemish painting, which was influential in Florence during the last quarter of the fifteenth century. Botticelli's late style, however, is apparent in the elongated form of the Virgin, whose bending body creates a sinuous S-shaped curve, and in her impulsive gesture as though fending off the Archangel Gabriel. The eurythmic movement of her hands is answered by the extended arm of Gabriel as it stabs the air. The suppleness of the body of Gabriel, sunk low on one knee, and the elegance of the Virgin's response activate the picture and animate what is otherwise a quiet and peaceful scene. There are some neat compositional tricks that reveal Botticelli's skill as a narrative painter, such as

the use of the patterned floor to draw the eye towards the landscape, the tree in the middle distance linking foreground to background, and the suggestion that the artist has waited until the very moment when Gabriel kneels so that he can incorporate the view beyond the room. The sense of space and the heaviness of the architectural elements are features that echo the designs of Giuliano da Sangallo, who built the church in which this altarpiece was placed.

15
LORENZO DI CREDI (1456–1536)
The Annunciation
88 × 71 cm, Galleria degli Uffizi, Florence

Lorenzo di Credi was trained in Verrocchio's workshop alongside Leonardo da Vinci who, together with Botticelli and Fra Bartolommeo, influenced his style. This *Annunciation* is one of his more lively and successful works, dating from *c*.1485. The scene is set in a high-ceilinged room beyond which is a landscape representing a *hortus conclusus* symbolizing the Virgin's chastity. The architectural elements of the interior are in a somewhat exaggerated Renaissance style of round arches, decorated pilasters, wide entablatures and circular windows in lunettes separated by smaller, paired, undecorated pilasters. Lorenzo di Credi has kept some distance between the Archangel Gabriel and the Virgin, which allows him to emphasize the landscape in the background. Below the Annunciation is a simulated predella where the artist has depicted related scenes from *Genesis*: the Creation of Eve, the Fall, and the Expulsion from Paradise. The painter prepared his composition meticulously with numerous drawings, paying close attention to draperies and facial expressions. The treatment of the landscape belies the extent of Flemish influence in Florentine painting towards the end of the fifteenth century.

16
GAUDENZIO FERRARI (1475/85–1546)
The Annunciation
88 × 86 cm, Gemäldegalerie Staatliche Museen Preussischer Kulturbesitz, Berlin

Gaudenzio Ferrari worked primarily in Lombardy, where he was heir to the Milanese tradition of Leonardo da Vinci, but quickly developed a mannerist style that formed the basis of early Lombard Baroque painting. It might seem that he was in some respects a transitional figure, but Gaudenzio Ferrari in fact painted a number of altarpieces and frescoes in a highly personal style that exerted an influence of its own. Not least, there are the paintings and sculptures he carried out for the chapels on the Sacro Monte near Varallo (*c*.1520–28), which are awe-inspiring and little known. *The Annunciation* dates from *c*.1512/13 and may once have formed part of an altarpiece. The artist provides a close-up of the scene observed from below. The light illuminates the faces sharply, and the slightly claustrophobic atmosphere suggests quiet but serious conversation; there is a sense of calm and deliberation. The Archangel Gabriel is shown not rushing towards the Virgin, but informing her with suitable gravity of her destiny. Swathes of drapery add to the feeling of immobility, just as the lily of unusually large size seems to burden Gabriel unnecessarily.

17
ANTONIAZZO ROMANO (IL CATALANO)
(documented 1461–1510)
The Annunciation
Santa Maria sopra Minerva, Rome

Antoniazzo Romano was the leading painter of the local school in Rome during the fifteenth century. The inability of the papacy to re-establish its supremacy in the city until fairly late on in the century meant that most of the major projects were undertaken by painters summoned especially to Rome. As a result, the Roman school of painting failed to establish its own identity. Antoniazzo Romano was not a painter of the first rank, but he was given many important commissions which he performed dutifully without a great deal of originality. His style was basically Umbrian, although his handling of light suggests that he had seen works by Piero della Francesca, who was in Rome in 1459. His *Annunciation* charms by its idiosyncrasies, notably the somewhat wobbly pose of the kneeling Virgin and the uncertainty in the drawing of the lectern. The Archangel Gabriel and the Virgin are made to appear larger than life-size in relation to the Dominican cardinal (Juan de Torquemada) and the three young girls he ushers forward to meet the Virgin. The girls are being assisted by the Virgin, who is giving each one of them a money bag. The artist carried out several works in Santa Maria sopra Minerva, and this panel was commissioned as the altarpiece for the chapel of the Confraternity of the Annunziata, formed in 1460 for helping girls without dowries. The participation of the cardinal gives this *Annunciation* an additional narrative interest.

18
ORAZIO GENTILESCHI (1562–1647)
The Annunciation
289 × 198 cm, Galleria Sabauda, Turin

The painting, long recognized as one of the artist's masterpieces, was given by Gentileschi to his patron Charles Emmanuel I, Duke of Savoy in 1623. The influence of Caravaggio is apparent not only in the light (both natural and divine) penetrating the room through the window situated high on the right, but also in the positioning of the Archangel Gabriel seen in three-quarters profile. The height of the room is emphasized by the vertical format and by the spectator's low viewpoint. The confrontation between the figures is quiet and subdued. There is an air of persuasion in Gabriel's pose and his pointing finger indicates the source of his mission. The muted colouring — blue, red and brown — is offset by the vivid white of the sheet on the bed. The room itself is rather impersonal, and great attention has been paid to the swathes of curtaining and to the draperies. Similarly, the sheet is rendered with a crispness and an eye for detail that is associated more with Dutch seventeenth-century painting. The feeling of tender intimacy in the picture emanates more from the suppression of emotion than from the detailing of numerous personal effects. The Virgin seems to sway gently in response to Gabriel's message, and the open palm of her right hand is the traditional gesture of welcome.

CORNELIS VAN POELENBURGH (c.1586–1667)
The Annunciation
48 × 41 cm, Kunsthistorisches Museum, Vienna

Cornelis van Poelenburgh was one of several Dutch artists who, during the early seventeenth century, spent a great deal of their working lives in Rome. Although born in Utrecht, where he later held influential positions in the art world, his style was mainly formed in Rome where he was in contact with Adam Elsheimer. Poelenburgh's work — which includes numerous landscapes, religious and mythological paintings — is on a small scale, often executed on copper and highly finished. Poelenburgh here seems to celebrate the Annunciation rather than merely to depict it. The viewer is only dimly conscious of the interior of the room, and the furnishings are reduced to a minimum. The distinction between the real and the visionary is clearly established. The Archangel Gabriel and the accompanying band of cherubim are veiled in cloud that fills the room. The Virgin understandably registers surprise at the manner of this unexpected intrusion. The door at the back of the room is unduly large, and to some extent creates an impression of the picture as the representation of a dream sequence.

The Nativity & the Holy Family

20

PIERO DELLA FRANCESCA (c.1416–1492)
Madonna del Parto
260 × 203 cm, Chapel of the Cemetery, Monterchi

Monterchi is a small village near where Tuscany merges into Umbria, lying between Città di Castello and Arezzo. To see this fresco of the pregnant Madonna demands something like a pilgrimage. The iconography is unique in Italian painting, although examples can be found in North European art. The artist's mother came from Monterchi, and it is possible that she was buried in the cemetery. Painted during the 1460s the depiction of a pregnant figure in a cemetery can be interpreted only as a symbol of life conquering death. The figure is seen like a sudden apparition, a contrived effect stage-managed by the two symmetrically-placed angels, one on either side drawing back the curtains. As Kenneth Clark once wrote of Piero della Francesca, 'No painter has shown more clearly the common foundations, in Mediterranean culture, of Christianity and paganism. His Madonna is the Great Mother, his risen Christ the slain god; his altar is set up on the threshing-floor, his saints have trodden grapes in the wine-press.'

21

HUGO VAN DER GOES (c.1440–1482)
The Adoration of the Shepherds
249 × 300 cm, Galleria degli Uffizi, Florence

This scene of *The Adoration of the Shepherds* was the centre of an extremely large altarpiece that was painted (c.1475) for Tommaso Portinari, the representative of the Medici family in Bruges. The wings of the altarpiece depict Tommaso Portinari and his two sons with SS. Anthony Abbot and Thomas (left), and Maria Portinari with her

daughter and SS. Margaret and Mary Magdalen (right). When the altarpiece was transported to Florence in 1483 it caused a sensation: several Florentine artists, including Domenico Ghirlandaio, were subject to its influence. The chief stylistic feature of the Portinari altarpiece is the simplicity of its overall design, which is contrasted by the close attention to detail in the actual application of paint. Everything in the altarpiece is involved in an act of adoration, the object of which is the small Christ Child lying naked on his back in front of the Virgin. Friedländer wrote, 'In the Portinari altarpiece a dualism is intensified to dramatic effect. The people — the "third estate", represented by the shepherds — press forward to salvation, and their rough lowliness, inspired with zealous faith, blends with the dignity of the saints and the lean spirituality of the angels so that the ultimate and supreme conception unites a richly contrasted community. With the shepherds a new kind of piety, drawn from the congregation, is devoted to the altarpiece, a coarse and lumbering rapture that is ennobled by emotion and touching devotion.' One of the most remarkable features of the altarpiece is the floral symbolism in the foreground, where fresh-cut flowers are placed in an *alabarello* (apothecary's jar) and a vase: these can be identified as lilies and irises, columbine and carnations. Scattered on the ground near by are violets. These spring flowers are specific symbols, but, more generally, they are in direct contrast with the winter landscape setting in which van der Goes correctly set *The Adoration of the Shepherds*. Their appearance out of season is a miraculous event to be equated with the appearance of God as man on earth in the form of the Christ Child. Shortly after painting the Portinari altarpiece Hugo van der Goes entered the monastery of Roodende, near Brussels, apparently not so much for religious reasons as because periodically he became mentally unbalanced and so needed the care of the monks.

22

FILIPPINO LIPPI (c.1457–1504)
The Nativity with two Angels
25 × 37 cm, National Gallery of Scotland, Edinburgh

A panel of this shape could only have been placed in the predella of an altarpiece, but no related panels are known and the location of the original altarpiece has also escaped identification. Limitations of space meant that artists were fairly restricted in the amount of detail that could be included in a predella panel. In addition, it was normally the function of the predella to complement the subject of the panels in the main part of the altarpiece. Filippino Lippi was the son of Filippo Lippi, but a more important influence on his style was Botticelli. It is from the example of this last painter that the bold rhythms of the composition, strong characterization of the figures, and vivid colouring are derived. A particularly striking effect in the painting is the rendering of the draperies of the two angels. The diaphanous material flutters behind them so that they seem more insubstantial than the Holy Family and appear to dance. They resemble the flames of flickering candles and are typical of Filippino Lippi's nervous, tense style. The Nativity takes place in the foreground, but the eye escapes into the background on both sides of the cleft of rock in the centre. The panel is often dated to the mid-1490s.

23

FOLLOWER OF JAN JOEST VAN CALCAR
(c.1455/60–1519)
The Nativity
101 × 70 cm, The Metropolitan Museum of Art, New York: the Jack and Belle Linsky Collection

A number of versions of this composition survive, and it is believed that they all follow from a nocturnal Nativity first devised by Hugo van der Goes. Jan Joest van Calcar was from Cleves in the lower Rhine region. There is some influence in his work of the Haarlem school, where he apparently set up a workshop by 1510 and spent the rest of his life. The principal source of illumination in the picture is the Christ Child lying in the crib: the light emanating from his body illuminates the faces of the Virgin and Joseph on the left, the angels kneeling in attendance and the two shepherds at the back. These last figures lean through a double-arched window divided by a porphyry column topped by a gilded pagan idol. Through the window in the landscape can be seen the Annunciation to the Shepherds beneath a sky streaked with the light of dawn. The painting is full of incident and atmosphere. A most engaging passage is the rendering of the infant angels at the top, who sing with their mouths wide open and with their hair flying in all directions providing an outburst of joy and musical sound — their efforts are such that their feet will surely end up by becoming twisted in the banderoles.

24

GEERTGEN TOT SINT JANS (c.1455/65–1485/95)
The Nativity at Night
34 × 25 cm, National Gallery, London

This is the earliest depiction of a Nativity in a nocturnal setting in the strict naturalistic meaning of the word. Two sources of artificial light penetrating the darkness are indicated: the fire in the left background lit by the shepherds in the field and the candle screened by Joseph's hand on the right reflected in his face. Both these sources are much reduced by the glow emanating from the angel arriving to guide the shepherds to Bethlehem, and the radiance from the Christ Child in the manger. Thus, supernatural light commingles with natural light, and it takes time for the viewer to adjust the eye and penetrate the shadows to discern the full range of the narrative. Geertgen's boldness in devising such a composition establishes a link between early Netherlandish art and Caravaggio, who exploited similar lighting effects to full advantage. The types painted by Geertgen are easily recognizable by their distinct facial features: rounded foreheads, tiny mouths and noses, receding chins and somewhat oriental eyes. In many respects there is a geometrical sense of form underlying these figures that suggests a process of simplification comparable with the work of Georges de la Tour. It is difficult to date this touching *Nativity* closely. Geertgen worked mainly in Leyden, and died before the age of thirty.

25

JACOPO TINTORETTO (1518–1594)
The Nativity
542 × 455 cm, Scuola di San Rocco, Venice

This vivid and energetic composition is part of an elaborate series of paintings decorating the Upper and Lower halls of the Scuola di San Rocco in Venice, which Tintoretto executed during the late 1570s and throughout the 1580s. *The Nativity* was painted between 1576 and 1581 and is located on the wall of the Upper Hall in a sequence illustrating scenes from the life of Christ which balances the Old Testament subjects depicted on the ceiling of this grandiose room. This scene is set in a spacious, but almost roofless, barn of which the artist shows us a view in section so that the viewer sees both upstairs and downstairs. The Holy Family is located in the more private quarters upstairs, while below the attendants and the shepherds share the space with the animals. It is not so much the poses or the grouping of the figures that unites the two halves of the composition as the light filtering through the broken rafters. Tintoretto enlivens the dark interior by strong accents of phosphorescent white on the draperies, and in doing so focuses attention on the Virgin and the Christ Child. The artist is entirely successful in creating what is essentially a rustic setting incorporating the warm straw and the farm implements. In such surroundings the event of Christ's birth is made to seem all the more remarkable. Perhaps only Rembrandt can rival Tintoretto's descriptive powers in this respect.

26

PETRUS CHRISTUS (c.1410–1472/3)
The Virgin and Child in a Gothic Interior
69.5 × 58 cm, The Nelson-Atkins Museum of Art, Kansas City. Nelson Fund

Paintings by Petrus Christus have a lucidity and finesse that offer comparisons with Dutch seventeenth-century art and even with Cubism. He was a close follower of Jan van Eyck, and may have worked in Italy and Spain. This *Virgin and Child* is a late work in which the artist emphasizes the plastic quality of the forms with the aid of clearly defined patterns of light and sharp contrasts of colour. The sheer perfection of the technique and composition is relieved only by the apple placed on the windowsill symbolizing the Fall of Man: this is balanced by the crystal orb held by the Christ Child, acknowledging his role as Salvator Mundi. Further back in the picture Joseph can be seen approaching. If anything, the high quality of the paintings by Petrus Christus has almost counted against him, as far as scholars are concerned; his search for purity of form has been criticized. Friedländer, for example, refers to the 'voluminous robes, which are reminiscent of armour in that they tell little of how the bodies are built, rather taking on balloon-like and tubular forms of their own'. The same writer regrettably concludes that Petrus Christus remains little more than a superb technician: 'His devotional and narrative approach is modest, frugal, and unassuming, but sometimes carries an admixture of sullen and humourless obduracy. The smooth brushwork of Petrus Christus, his deep and harmonious colour schemes (at times on the dull side to be sure), in which browns and maroons predominate, the vigour with which he shapes interiors and models his figures — all these more than make up for a certain pettiness and limited vocabulary of form.'

27

MASTER OF THE MAGDALEN LEGEND
(c.1483–1527)
The Holy Family
65 × 52 cm, Koninklijk Museum voor Schone Kunsten, Antwerp

The identity of the artist has not been established, but he was active in Brussels c.1500. The appellation is taken from the scenes of the life of St Mary Magdalen that once formed a triptych (1515–20) and are now divided between various collections. The composition is clearly retardataire, but the artist enlivens it with anecdotal detail. The Virgin's sewing basket lies by the stool, indicating her occupation before the arrival of Joseph, who makes his way into the room carrying a basket full of his carpentry tools. He walks with a stick and holds a pair of spectacles as though to survey the scene. Liveliest of all is the Christ Child, who tugs at Joseph's cloak and indicates his mother. It is a totally domestic scene, as though father is returning from work, but no less enchanting for its mundane, prosaic treatment. It is also in stark contrast with the tragic events that are to befall the small, eager Child.

28

PETER PAUL RUBENS (1577–1640)
The Holy Family under the Apple Tree with SS. John the Baptist, Elizabeth and Zacharias
353 × 233 cm, Kunsthistorisches Museum, Vienna

This panel formed part of one of the artist's largest and most impressive altarpieces, painted between 1620 and 1622 for the Brotherhood of St Idelphonsus. It was placed in the Lady Chapel of the church of St Jacques sur Coudenberg in Brussels. The Brotherhood was founded by Archduke Albert as a lay association for Hapsburg courtiers. The altarpiece was paid for by the Archduke's widow in his memory. It remained in the church until 1777, when it was bought by Queen Maria Theresa of Austria. The central panel depicted the Virgin giving St Idelphonsus a set of vestments. This was flanked by images of the two regents being presented by their patron saints (Albert of Louvain and Elizabeth of Hungary). On the reverse of these panels Rubens painted *The Holy Family under the Apple Tree*; this was originally in two halves, which have now been joined together for modern display. The whole structure may be seen as the culmination of the medieval tradition of altarpieces. The imagery serves a dual purpose being both typical and symbolic: in the biblical *Song of Solomon* (2:3), for example, the King is compared with an apple tree under whose branches the beloved sits. The altarpiece was an immensely prestigious commission, and Rubens expended a great deal of effort on it. Dating from the start of the final decade of his life, the mastery over drawing, light, texture and composition is consummate. Few painters had the power and ability to put on such a display of visual pyrotechnics over which the eye ranges with ever increasing delight.

29

REMBRANDT VAN RIJN (1606–1669)
The Holy Family
41 × 34 cm, Musée du Louvre, Paris

Rembrandt painted the Virgin suckling the Christ Child only twice in his whole career (the other representation is in Munich), and on both occasions he created an overwhelming feeling of domestic bliss. This painting is dated 1640 and, like its counterpart in Munich, may have been painted specifically upon commission. The Christ Child is illuminated by light entering the room through the window on the left, where Joseph is at work with his carpentry. The rest of the picture is a detailed depiction of an interior with a large fireplace that dominates the right. During the eighteenth century the picture was known affectionately as *The Household of the Furniture-worker*, and such paintings by Rembrandt had a pronounced influence on nineteenth-century European art. There is no indication of divinity, and Rembrandt penetrates to the very core of family life — one of the many moods that he could evoke so successfully in his paintings, drawings and prints.

30

PIETER FRANSZ DE GREBBER (c.1600–1652/3)
The Virgin Teaching the Christ Child to Read
95.5 × 74 cm, Musée des Beaux-Arts, Quimper

The subject is not recorded in the bible and is apocryphal, forming part of the cycle of events that are imagined to have taken place while the Holy Family was in exile in Egypt. A parallel scene in the Virgin's own life (St Anne teaching the Virgin to read) is sometimes depicted by artists. On the whole, however, it is a comparatively rare subject in painting, although the theme is found more commonly in manuscripts of earlier centuries. Painters of the seventeenth century responded more readily to the idea. Grebber worked in Haarlem and was trained within the Flemish mannerist tradition, although he was open to more commanding influences such as Rubens, Jordaens, Hals and Rembrandt. His style is recognizable by its accurate drawing, subdued palette (grey, mauve, rose) and gentle lighting. Such stylistic features are perfectly in accord with the subject of this picture, which the artist has invested with a poetic dignity. The profile of the Virgin, the caressing light and the soft tonality evoke a domestic calm that lifts what is basically a *genre* subject to the religious level. The figures are not equated with the ideal, but are seen as a normal mother and child: there are no indications of divinity. Like Rembrandt, Grebber made his religious paintings appear to be an extension of everyday life.

The Magi

31

GIOTTO DI BONDONE (1276–1337)
The Epiphany
44.9 × 43.7 cm, The Metropolitan Museum of Art, New York. John Stewart Kennedy Fund

The panel is one of a series probably dating from the early 1320s illustrating scenes from the life of Christ. Six related panels are known: *The Presentation in the Temple* (Gardner Museum, Boston), *The Entombment*

(Villa I Tatti, Florence, Berenson Collection), *Pentecost* (National Gallery, London), *Last Supper*, *Crucifixion*, and *Christ in Limbo* (all in Alte Pinakothek, Munich). No doubt there were other panels to complete the series, but exactly how many has not been determined; neither is it certain how all the scenes would originally have been arranged. It is often assumed that they were part of an altarpiece. The fact that St Francis is shown kneeling at the foot of the cross in the *Crucifixion* suggests that the panels originally came from a Franciscan church. The dimensions are fairly small, but it is characteristic of Giotto that he invests the figures with a feeling of monumentality and creates firmly demarcated spatial intervals within a confined area. Giotto's attention to detail in the modelling of the faces and draperies is of the highest quality. Two iconographic aspects are worth noting. Firstly, the disposition of the Virgin reclining in the stable is derived from the Byzantine tradition by which she is shown in a cave. Secondly, it is most unusual for one of the Magi to be depicted lifting the Christ Child from the manger. Giotto has compressed the narrative to include the Nativity, the Adoration of the Magi and, in the left background, the Annunciation to the Shepherds.

32
THEODORIC (active mid-fourteenth century)
The Adoration of the Kings (detail)
Kreuzkappelle, Karlstejn Castle

The Adoration of the Kings is a fresco in the Chapel of the Holy Cross in Karlstejn Castle in Bohemia. It forms part of an extensive scheme of decoration including panel paintings and frescoes on the walls of the Chapel, carried out between 1357 and 1367. The Chapel is, in fact, the greatest surviving example of Gothic painting in Czechoslovakia. The artist responsible for the work was Master Theodoric, who is first recorded in Prague in 1359, when he is also referred to as court painter to Charles IV. The origins of Theodoric's style are not known, and it is difficult to determine how he developed the characteristics displayed in his paintings for the Chapel of the Holy Cross. Admittedly, there are Italian and Franco-Flemish parallels for the conception of form and the attempt at spatial organization, but this does not necessarily mean that Theodoric knew such work at first hand. Theodoric's own style is recognizable by the rounded forms, pudgy features, almost jointless limbs, grey-toned modelling and subdued colouring. The panels in the Chapel are ranged in rows on the walls and in the window recesses. Those on the altar wall are centred thematically and literally on the scene of the Crucifixion. The other walls contain a whole cast of saints, bishops, monks, nuns and ecclesiastics. The iconography of the chapel was inspired by the Book of *Revelation* and is intended to represent the New Jerusalem on earth. Similar schemes are known in Italy. The fresco of *The Adoration of the Kings* is found on the southern side of the window recess on the east wall. Although Theodoric employed a team of associates to carry out the work in the chapel, this fresco is autographed.

33
MASTER OF LIESBORN (active second half of the fifteenth century)
The Adoration of the Child and *The Adoration of the Kings*
each 58.5 × 37.5 cm, Westfälisches Landesmuseum für Kunst und Kulturgeschichte, Münster

The Master of Liesborn is so named after the high altarpiece that was commissioned by Abbot Heinrich von Kleve for the Benedictine monastery at Liesborn in Westphalia (Germany). The altarpiece, which was probably in the form of a triptych, was apparently finished in 1465, but was removed from the monastery in the early nineteenth century and dismembered. Parts of the central panel are in the National Gallery, London. The artist was strongly influenced by the Cologne school of painting and his work displays knowledge of the Netherlandish school. He ran an active workshop responsible for painting many altarpieces, including one for the monastery at Herzebrock in Westphalia which shows eight scenes from the life of the Virgin in the shutters. The present scenes are two of those from the left shutter. The central panel of the altarpiece is lost, but it is thought that the subject represented was the Virgin as Queen of Heaven.

34
PETER PAUL RUBENS (1577–1640)
The Adoration of the Kings
447 × 336 cm, Koninklijk Museum voor Schone Kunsten, Antwerp

Rubens painted this magnificent altarpiece in 1624 for the church of St Michael, Antwerp. It is a towering composition in which the artist crowds figures together to create a feeling of excitement and anticipation. Such altarpieces were prepared by means of many drawings, extending from sketches of the whole design to detailed studies of individual figures, and finally through a *modello*. The kings and the members of their entourage are vividly characterized. It is also unusual for the Virgin to be shown standing, as though introducing the Christ Child to the visitors. The painter made a few changes from the arrangement of the figures in the *modello*: as finally depicted, the Virgin now faces more towards the viewer and the two kings in the foreground. The Corinthian column is also an addition. The actual painting of the altarpiece was extremely rapid — the surface is thinly spread, involving only undermodelling and one other layer. This rapidity of execution gives the altarpiece a spontaneity and fluency that is just as evident in the use of colour.

The Flight into Egypt

35
JEAN-HONORÉ FRAGONARD (1732–1806)
The Rest on the Flight into Egypt
67 × 57 cm, Baltimore Museum of Art: the Mary Frick Jacobs Collection

This is a youthful work by Fragonard, undertaken while he was still being trained in the studio of François Boucher (1748–1752) and before he won the Prix de Rome and went to study in Italy. Not surprisingly, Fragonard's early paintings are influenced by those of Boucher, particularly in the

light palette and the type of composition favoured for allegorical subject-matter, but a great deal of the young artist's time was also spent in copying the old masters. *The Rest on the Flight into Egypt* does not seem to have been copied, but it is very much in the tradition of seventeenth-century Italian painting. It is interesting that Fragonard favours the use of diagonals even though the format is circular. Cleverly he contrives to place the Christ Child in the centre by making the Virgin hold him up in a playful way. Joseph seems more concerned with the safety of his charges. Fragonard almost conceals the group in cloud, as though the viewer is witnessing a vision. The interpretation is unusual and effective, anticipating Fragonard's greater freedom in the treatment of subject-matter at a later date. Other religious pictures of these early years include *The Visitation* and *The Education of the Virgin*.

36
GIOTTO DI BONDONE (1276–1337)
The Flight into Egypt
200 × 185 cm, Capella degli Scrovegni (Arena Chapel), Padua

Giotto worked in the Arena Chapel at Padua between 1302 and 1305 during which time he painted an extensive series of frescoes around the walls depicting the story of Joachim and Anna, the early life of the Virgin, and the life of Christ, reaching a climax in the *Last Judgement* on the entrance wall. The Arena Chapel was private: it was built by Enrico Scrovegni. The building derived its name from the Roman arena that was near by, but the chapel was in fact dedicated first of all to Santa Maria della Carità and then a few years later to Santa Maria Annunziata. The frescoes are justly celebrated as one of the watersheds of European art, and nowhere is Giotto's prowess more apparent than in *The Flight into Egypt*. The composition is so arranged that the pyramidal shape of the Virgin and Child riding on the donkey is echoed by the mountain behind them; the action flows steadily from left to right. Even though the figures complement the setting Giotto depicts an essentially hostile landscape. There is, for instance, a precipitous drop in the foreground, as the group hastens on through the mountains towards its destination. One of the strengths of Giotto's art is his broad range of characterization. This is not a stately procession, but people fleeing in fear of their lives. So Giotto quickens the rhythm by making Joseph in the lead look back to check on the well-being of his family, while opposite the servants point the way forward and stride out so as not to lose contact.

37
VITTORE CARPACCIO (c.1460–1523/6)
The Flight into Egypt
72 × 111.5 cm, National Gallery of Art, Washington D.C.: the Andrew W. Mellon Collection

Painting c.1500, Carpaccio has set this *Flight into Egypt* in an open landscape full of anecdotal detail. The boat on the river in the left half of the composition may form part of the narrative, in that the journey to Egypt involved crossing rivers and lakes, although this was an aspect of the story cherished mainly by seventeenth-century painters. The figures in the foreground are conceived on a monumental scale. Joseph strides out urging the donkey on, while the Virgin gently supports the Child. The decorative quality of the Virgin's drapery and the dependence on landscape are characteristic of Venetian painters. The firm and accurate drawing of the figures is an important feature of Carpaccio's art.

38
JOOS VAN CLEVE (c.1464–1540)
The Rest on the Flight into Egypt
54 × 67.5 cm, Musées Royaux des Beaux-Arts, Brussels

Joos van Cleve carried the tradition of David and Memlinc (both of Bruges) into the sixteenth century. He seems also to have been influenced by Massys and Patinir (both of Antwerp), as well as by Leonardo da Vinci. This *Rest on the Flight into Egypt* follows the interpretation depicted by David, but evokes far more the atmosphere of a picnic than that of a critical moment in a tense drama. As Friedländer wrote, 'Joos may not enter deeply into the tragic aspects of the Christian faith, but celebrates the bliss of the Virgin all the more jubilantly . . .' There is a fairy-tale feeling about the landscape. 'Perspective, foreshortening, the graduation in the scale within the background — all these served the painter less to project the infinity of space than to make the figures to the fore appear all the larger, in contrast to the fussy detail of the virtually independent background. Zigzag lines blaze a trail from the greenish-brown foreground to the pale blue distances. Crumbling, mossy rocks alternate with dark masses of foliage. Grotesque crags rise obliquely in the middle ground . . . while behind them hills, rivers, bridges, paths, houses and mills form a panorama seen in geographical perspective.'

39
JOACHIM PATINIR (c.1485–1524)
The Rest on the Flight into Egypt
121 × 177 cm, Museo del Prado, Madrid

Philip II of Spain owned four important late works by Patinir that are still in Madrid. Rather than concentrating on the group of the Holy Family, the artist has decided to emphasize the setting in order to heighten the sense of drama. The landscape may at first sight appear to serve as a mere backdrop, but in fact it teems with incidents pertaining to the subject of the picture. The Virgin suckles the Child on a hillock in the foreground. In front of her are the Holy Family's meagre belongings. Joseph is seen in the middle distance on the left; he has been to fetch water. Dangers lie around: behind the Virgin in the wood a man can be seen loading a crossbow. On the left is a town inhabited by Bosch-like figures: statues topple to the ground while a goose is sacrificed before a snouted figure. On the right, beyond where the donkey grazes, there is a depiction of rustic activity. Much of this imagery is an expression of the symbolic significance of Christ's birth as recounted in texts such as *The Golden Legend* of Jacobus de Voragine. For example, just to the right of the Virgin are the remains of a classical altar, which the new religion will replace; and on the left a vine can be seen growing round the trunk of a tree — clearly a reference to the Passion.

40
GERARD DAVID (c.1460–1523)
The Rest on the Flight into Egypt
44.3 × 44.9 cm, National Gallery of Art, Washington D.C.: the Andrew W. Mellon Collection

A comparatively late work (c.1510), this painting is based upon the account of the journey to Egypt given in the apocryphal *Gospel of Pseudo-Matthew* (chapters 20/21). According to this source, when the Holy Family rested on the journey the Christ Child commanded a palm tree to give forth fruit from one of its branches and water from beneath its roots. Joseph is shown evidently collecting food on the right of the composition — although the tree is not obviously a palm — and a stream can be made out in the lower right corner of the picture. The bunch of grapes from which the Christ Child is eating, symbolizing the Passion, appears to have been brought along in the Virgin's hamper. In the context of the Passion the palm tree can also be interpreted symbolically. Such subject-matter encouraged artists to treat the theme of the Rest on the Flight as a pastoral scene. The accurate drawing of the Virgin's facial features and the intricate folds of the drapery are highly characteristic of Netherlandish painting at this date.

41
ORAZIO GENTILESCHI (1562–1647)
The Rest on the Flight into Egypt
175.3 × 218.4 cm,
Birmingham Museums and Art Gallery

Gentileschi was a Tuscan by birth, who went to Rome towards the end of the sixteenth century and came under the influence of Caravaggio's early style. It is the spirit of Caravaggio which dominates this large and boldly conceived composition painted by Gentileschi during the second decade of the seventeenth century, even though there is some residual Tuscan influence in the treatment of the Virgin. The sharp lighting and the realistic treatment of the theme reveal the impact of Caravaggio. It is clear that the Holy Family have been forced to rest for the night in the open air. Only a wall provides the barest protection from the elements and on the other side of this wall the artist has placed the donkey whose head is silhouetted against the sky. By this device Gentileschi has provided himself with the opportunity to concentrate on the figures which he has painted with the greatest conviction. There are very few poses in art more startling than that given to the aged Joseph lying back exhausted after the long journey and it could well have been inspired by Caravaggio's painting of *The Conversion of St Paul* in the church of S. Maria del Popolo, Rome, dating from 1600–1. Ultimately, however, it is the figure of the Virgin suckling the Christ Child that commands attention and forms a telling contrast with the plight of the Holy Family escaping from Herod.

42
ANTHONY VAN DYCK (1599–1641)
The Rest on the Flight into Egypt
134.5 × 114.5 cm, Alte Pinakothek, Munich

The figures are placed on a diagonal emphasized by the sprawling body of the sleeping Christ Child. The composition was almost certainly inspired by

Italian, specifically Venetian, examples which van Dyck had seen while in Italy c.1621–27: a date shortly after 1627 is normally proposed for this painting. The relationship between the Virgin and Child is wonderfully and simply expressed, a pyramid of human warmth painted with great fluency. The landscape, too, has remarkable freshness and a dexterity of brushwork that anticipates later centuries. The picture has suffered some damage, most evidently in the blue of the Virgin's drapery. The canvas itself has been extended at the upper edge by about 20 cm.

43
ADRIAEN VAN DER WERFF (1659–1722)
The Rest on the Flight into Egypt
54.5 × 43 cm, National Gallery, London

Adriaen van der Werff was the most esteemed Dutch painter of his time, and he reaped considerable financial advantages from his success. He lived most of his life in Rotterdam, but his fame sprang from his employment in 1697 by the Elector Palatine. As court painter, van der Werff had to work for the Elector for six months of the year; from 1703 this was increased to nine months. His style is based on the tradition of the school of Leyden, but there is also an element of French classical influence detectable in his pictures. Contemporaries admired the high finish of his style and the smooth application of paint. Adriaen van der Werff's interpretation of *The Rest on the Flight into Egypt* is a fine example of his style. The Child is bathed in a soft light while the Virgin and Joseph are left in darker areas of half-light. The sense of urgency or anxiety in the biblical story has here evaporated. The world of Antoine Watteau and the *fête champêtre* is not difficult to detect, whereas the Christ Child seems more closely related to mythology than to scripture. The technical perfection of the picture is admirable, but the characterization is perhaps too sweet.

The Presentation & Circumcision

44
ANDREA MANTEGNA (1430/1–1506)
The Presentation of Christ in the Temple
69 × 86.3 cm, Gemäldegalerie Staatliche Museen Preussischer Kulturbesitz, Berlin

The figures are seen in half-length contained within an illusionistic frame of coloured marble. It is possible that Mantegna was the first to devise this type of composition, which was also adopted by his brother-in-law Giovanni Bellini; it was almost certainly inspired by antique relief sculpture. Mantegna, however, has been careful to avoid a flat row of figures. The young Virgin, holding the Child, and Simeon face one another in the front plane, while the aged Joseph is seen full-face, no doubt inspired by an antique sculptured portrait. These principal figures are offset against the dark background by the haloes and the dramatic treatment of light. The Virgin and Simeon are painted in a particularly striking way: both wear beautiful brocades, but youthfulness is tellingly balanced by old age. Behind this main group are two figures, one at either edge of the painting. On the left is the artist's wife, Nicolosia, and on the right the painter himself. They were married in 1453, but in view of the nature of the subject, it is likely that the picture was painted slightly later as a votive offering for the safe birth of their first child.

45
GIOVANNI BELLINI (c.1430–1516)
The Circumcision
75 × 102 cm, National Gallery, London

The frieze-like composition of half-length figures resembles that of the *Presentation of the Virgin* adopted at an earlier date by Mantegna. The effect of Bellini's compact and coherent grouping around an altar at which the circumcision is performed owes less to sculpture. The figures are disposed in more of a semicircle, and in this respect the illusion of depth is more nearly related to Bellini's altarpieces than to ancient reliefs. The light enters the picture from the left, but the faces of the female figures on the right also appear to be lit from below. Seen against a dark background, the treatment of light unifies the composition and at the same time creates an atmosphere of religious awe that suits the occasion. The Virgin supports the Child on the right. The modelling of her face and the crumpled texture of the drapery are typical of Bellini's softer style of painting, evolved during the last decade of the fifteenth century. The composition was frequently imitated by Bellini's studio assistants and followers.

The Madonna & Child

46
CIMABUE (CENNI DI PEPPI) (c.1240–after 1302)
The Virgin and Child Enthroned, Surrounded by Angels
427 × 280 cm, Musée du Louvre, Paris

This large, gabled altarpiece was originally in the church of San Francesco, Pisa, where it was seen by Vasari in the sixteenth century. It belongs to a group of altarpieces of similar proportions which includes Cimabue's panel once in Santa Trinita, Florence (now in the Uffizi) and Duccio's Ruccellai Madonna, once in Santa Maria Novella, Florence (now also in the Uffizi), both dating from the 1280s. The effect of these altarpieces is imposing, mainly because of the scale. The figures are almost twice life-size, and were evidently painted to be seen from a distance. The intention was to create a sense of awe, and for this purpose the artist has deliberately chosen a simple but significant design that sees the Virgin and Child raised on a carved wooden throne supported by three angels symmetrically placed on each side. For painters who so frequently worked in fresco this enlarged scale did not pose particular problems. Care has been taken with the modelling of the flesh, the carving of the throne (that would not have been out of place in Hollywood during the 1920s or 1930s) and the colouring of the angels' wings. The whole composition seems so solidly based that it is difficult to realize that the throne and the angels are actually airborne and that the gold background is representative of heaven. The panel probably dates from c.1300 and seems to have some influence of the Sienese painter Duccio. The frame is decorated with twenty-six medallions containing images of prophets, saints and angels.

47
DUCCIO DI BUONINSEGNA (active 1278–1318/19)
The Virgin and Child with two Angels
89 × 60 cm, Museo dell' Opera della Metropolitana, Siena

Widely regarded as an early work by Duccio (c.1280), this *Virgin and Child* is known as the Crevole Madonna after the small town near Siena where it was discovered. The composition combines old and new in a remarkable way. The pose of the Christ Child extending his hand up to grasp the Virgin's mantle is a motif that occurs for the first time (possibly in this very picture) in paintings of the late thirteenth century and helps to make the relationship between mother and child more natural. In addition, Duccio manages to give the figures a psychological dimension that establishes a rapport with the viewer. This is achieved by means of a commanding technical skill, above all in a sensitivity to line and to colour, that had not been attained in art before. In the Crevole Madonna we can witness the shift from the hieratic conception of the Virgin and Child to a more humane understanding and representation of the divine. The modelling of the flesh tones on the Virgin's face and the firm outline of her body against the gold background reveal a craftsman of extraordinary skill.

48
TADDEO DI BARTOLO (c.1362–1422)
Head of the Virgin
19.7 × 13.7 cm, The Metropolitan Museum of Art, New York: the Robert Lehman Collection

Taddeo di Bartolo was a prolific and fairly influential Sienese painter, who was trained within the fourteenth-century tradition emanating from Simone Martini. He was, however, a transitional figure who helped to introduce Renaissance principles into Sienese art. The chief virtue of his style lay in powerful drawing which, in turn, led to a vigorous narrative most evident in his predella panels and frescoes. This is a fragment from a larger painting. Two other fragments of heads of angels are in the same collection. Seen out of context like this the *Head of the Virgin* has the directness of a primitive painting such as the funerary portraits made by the Egyptians, or an icon.

49
TADDEO DI BARTOLO (c.1362–1422)
The Virgin and Child
100.3 × 68 cm, Philbrook Art Center, Tulsa

In this *Virgin and Child* the formal pose of the Virgin is to some extent undermined by the playful attitude of the Child. The panel has a pronounced vertical axis — an effect exaggerated by the wings of the cherubim — and almost certainly once formed the centre of a large altarpiece.

50
MASTER OF THE ST VERDIANA PANEL (active c.1390–1415)
The Virgin and Child with Saints
80.7 × 54.3 cm, High Museum of Art, Atlanta. Gift of the Samuel H. Kress Foundation

This anonymous artist was a follower of the Florentine painter, Agnolo Gaddi. His appellation is derived from this panel, in which along with SS.

Nicholas, Catherine of Alexandria, Anthony Abbot, Julian and Dorothy, the named saint is shown with her attribute of two snakes. According to hagiographical tradition, the saint disliked snakes but in the cause of mortifying the flesh allowed them to molest her. St Verdiana is the patron saint of Castelfiorentino, a town near Florence. The painter has shown the Madonna dell' Umiltà appearing to the saints as though in a vision. A date c.1390 is likely for this work.

51
GENTILE DA FABRIANO (c.1370–1427)
The Virgin and Child with SS. Julian and Lawrence
90.8 × 47 cm, The Frick Collection, New York

This small altarpiece was painted while Gentile da Fabriano was in Florence, at about the same time as the Strozzi altarpiece (*Adoration of the Kings* in the Uffizi) of 1423 and the Quaratesi polyptych (centre panel of *The Virgin and Child* in the Royal Collection) of 1425. Clearly the present altarpiece was executed for an important patron, but a specific identification has not yet been made. It is likely, however, that this altarpiece would have been painted for a private chapel in the household of a leading family. The composition demonstrates the development of Gentile da Fabriano's manner of painting away from the International Gothic style that he had adopted at the outset of his career. The artist's main preoccupation here is with spatial organization. The figures form a triangle. The kneeling saints are carefully positioned with regard to the Virgin, and the Christ Child's sudden movement helps to unite the upper and lower halves of the composition. So important has the representation of space become that Gentile da Fabriano adjusts the haloes of the two saints to avoid disturbing their profiles. The colour is another significant aspect of the altarpiece: the bright orange cloth of honour offsets the blue of the Virgin's cloak and the elegantly embroidered garments worn by the Christ Child and the two saints. As though to intensify the colours, Gentile da Fabriano bathes the figures in an intense light that enters the picture from the right.

52
GENTILE DA FABRIANO (c.1370–1427)
The Virgin and Child
110.4 × 66.3 cm, Museo Capitolare, Velletri

This much damaged painting was commissioned by Cardinal Ardicino della Porta to celebrate the nine-hundredth anniversary of the founding of the church of SS. Cosma and Damiano, Rome. Although disfigured, the panel has passages of high quality, as in the modelling of the faces and in the use of colour to offset the figures. The sense of monumentality and the tendency to simplify are indications that this is a late work by the artist. 'The Velletri *Madonna and Child* thus testifies to an expansion of means and a more concrete expressive goal' (Christiansen). The effect is sculptural. The iconography of the Virgin seated on the ground is known as the Madonna dell' Umiltà, which was introduced into Italian art during the mid-fourteenth century and was often used by Sienese painters.

53

AMBROGIO LORENZETTI (active 1319–1348)
*The Virgin and Child with Angels, SS. Dorothy,
Catherine of Alexandria and the Doctors of the Church*
50.5 × 34.5 cm, Pinacoteca Nazionale, Siena

The fortunes of this small, portable altarpiece
(known as the Little Maestà) have fluctuated
dramatically. Having once been described as 'a little
masterpiece, perhaps the most beautiful painting by
Ambrogio', it has been considered by one writer
instead to be a pastiche of Lorenzettian motifs
assembled by a fifteenth-century painter. Most
scholars, however, now accept the altarpiece as a late
work (c.1340) by Ambrogio Lorenzetti, who
possessed all the refinement of hue and colour
associated with the tradition of Duccio, but
supplemented it with a sense of volume and form
derived from Giotto and contemporary sculpture.
The results are powerful and commanding, with a
strong narrative exemplified by the frescoes of *Good
and Bad Government* in the Palazzo Pubblico, Siena.
Lorenzetti's powers of organization are apparent here
in the vivid patterning of the carpet that covers the
steps of the throne, leading the eye towards the
Virgin and Child, or the way in which the angels
form an arch following the contours of the panel.
Similarly, the saints are disposed around the throne
so that they enhance the feeling of the physical
presence of the Virgin and Child. The figures have
monumentality even on this reduced scale. The vivid
colours, rich brocades, and gold tooling create a
dazzling jewel-like effect. St Dorothy is on the left,
carrying roses; St Catherine of Alexandria on the
right, holding her wheel. The papal saints in the
immediate foreground are Clement and Gregory;
and the two bishop saints behind may be Nicholas
and Martin.

54

PIETRO LORENZETTI (active 1305–1348)
The Virgin and Child with Angels
145 × 122 cm, Galleria degli Uffizi, Florence

Pietro Lorenzetti's art shares the same characteristics
as those of his brother, Ambrogio, and both almost
certainly died in the Black Death plague of 1348.
This altarpiece is signed and dated 1340: it was
formerly in the church of San Francesco, Pistoia,
where it was seen by Vasari who noted that it had a
predella. The altarpiece is notable for its symmetrical
arrangement of the angels around a somewhat flimsy
throne. The Virgin's body is succinctly prescribed
by the elegant swathes of drapery dropping straight
to the floor on one side and passing across the knee
on the other. This disposition of the drapery reveals a
sense of form that anticipates Piero della Francesca
and is one of the most arresting passages of painting
in fourteenth-century Italian art: the eye plays
endlessly upon the cascading edges that almost
entrap the Virgin within the spacious throne.

55

SIMONE MARTINI (c.1284–1344)
The Virgin and Child
67.5 × 48.3 cm, The Metropolitan Museum of Art,
New York: the Robert Lehman Collection

Formerly attributed to Lippo Vanni, this panel was
part of a polyptych from which related parts
depicting half-length figures of saints are known.
Simone Martini's style, with its gently undulating
outlines and strong iridescent colours, epitomises
Sienese painting of the early fourteenth century.
Every part of the panel is carefully executed, not least
the gold background, the punched haloes and the
bands of decoration prescribing the edges. It should
be recalled that at the time such panels were painted,
the only form of illumination was candlelight so that
strong colours offset by the gold background gave
the work a jewel-like glow in the darkness.

56

FRA ANGELICO (c.1395–1455)
*The Virgin and Child with Angels
(central panel from a triptych)*
260 × 330 cm, Museo di San Marco, Florence

The altarpiece, of which this painting forms the
central panel, is known as the Linaiuoli triptych.
The name is derived from its original commission in
1433 by the Guild of Flax-workers (Arte dei
Linaiuoli) as a work to be set up in their guild-hall
situated on the Piazza Sant' Andrea in Florence. It
also happens to be an altarpiece of exceptionally
large dimensions, almost certainly the largest in mid-
fifteenth century Florence, and really only
comparable with altarpieces dating from the
thirteenth century. The marble tabernacle in which
the Linaiuoli triptych is set was designed by the
sculptor Lorenzo Ghiberti, whose influence can also
be detected in the figures on the two-sided folding
wings. On the inside of the wings are SS. John the
Evangelist and John the Baptist; on the outside SS.
Mark and Peter. The scale of these saints is so great
that it is clear that Fra Angelico was emulating the
monumental sculptured figures by Ghiberti and
Donatello on the outside of the church of Or San
Michele in Florence, which were also commissioned
by various guilds. There were narrative scenes in the
predella. The central panel of the triptych is one of
Angelico's most celebrated works. The Christ
Child seems more like a small boy than a baby, and
is shown standing with an orb in his left hand
referring to his role as *Salvator Mundi*. The music-
making angels in the wooden frame surrounding the
Virgin and Child are still the most popular figures
in the whole of Angelico's oeuvre.

57

FRA ANGELICO (c.1395–1455)
The Virgin and Child
100 × 60 cm, Galleria Sabauda, Turin

The low posture of the Virgin suggests a comparison
with the iconography of the Madonna dell' Umiltà,
but she is in fact seated on a marble throne which is
in the style of Michelozzo, who designed the
monastery of San Marco in Florence. The painting
is late (c.1450). Apart from the architecture, a feeling
of luxury is induced by the quality of the brocades
and the darker palette.

58

FILIPPO LIPPI (c.1406–1469)
The Adoration of the Child
129.5 × 118.5 cm, Gemäldegalerie Staatliche
Museen Preussischer Kulturbesitz, Berlin

This *Adoration of the Child* served as the altarpiece for
the chapel in the Palazzo Medici, Florence, the walls
of which were frescoed by Benozzo Gozzoli with the
scene of *The Adoration of the Magi*. The altarpiece
dates from the mid-1450s. The iconography is
unusual because of the woodland setting, but the
artist adopted it on other occasions. On the central
axis at the top of the panel immediately above the
Christ Child are God the Father and the Holy
Ghost. To the left are St Bernard, kneeling in prayer
behind a rock, and in the middle distance the
standing figure of St John the Baptist, who holds a
banner inscribed *Ecce Agnus Dei*. In the lower left
corner is a tree stump with an axe embedded in it,
the shaft of which is inscribed with the artist's name.
On the right in the middle distance is a stork with a
snake in its beak. Most of these images have
symbolic meanings: the axe in the tree stump alludes
to the biblical quotation 'And now also the axe is
laid unto the root of the tree: therefore every tree
which bringeth not forth good fruit is hewn down,
and cast into the fire' (MATTHEW 3:10); and the
stork eating the serpent represents Christ overcoming
evil. It is the setting, however, that pervades the
picture with a mystical element comparable with
such texts as the *Revelations* of St Bridget. The
overall theme is therefore one of penitence treated
within the context of medieval mysticism. A similar
mood can be detected in Netherlandish painting of
the same date (for example, Rogier van der
Weyden), although here Lippi paints the forest so
successfully that to a modern viewer it seems almost a
romantic conception of *The Adoration of the Child*.

59

FRANCESCO DI STEFANO PESELLINO
(c.1422–1457)
Virgin and Child with Six Saints
26.4 × 23.8 cm, The Metropolitan Museum of Art,
New York. Bequest of Mary Stillman Harkness

Pesellino was a contemporary of Fra Angelico and
collaborated with Filippo Lippi, but few of his
works have survived. Regardless of the losses, he is
recognized today as an important artist of the early
Renaissance in Florence trying to solve problems of
space and volume within the traditional formulae of
religious painting. The present painting is on a small
scale and Pesellino has adopted a miniaturist style.
An altarpiece of these dimensions is more likely to
have been placed in a private chapel in a domestic
context than in a large church. Pesellino's skill can
be appreciated by the fact that, even on this reduced
scale, the figures are invested with a feeling of
monumentality, and are vividly characterized.
Compositionally, it is fascinating to see how the
artist has positioned the saints around the Virgin and
Child without allowing them to overwhelm the
central group. Rather, the balanced distribution of
these figures on either side of the throne, and the
different levels of their heads, help to draw the
viewer's eye towards the Virgin and Child. The
male saints can be identified as SS. Anthony Abbot
and Jerome (on the left) and SS. Augustine and
George (on the right). The female saints at the back
may be Cecilia and Catherine of Alexandria
respectively, but these identifications are less certain.

60

FRANCESCO DI STEFANO PESELLINO
(c.1422–1457)
The Virgin and Child with the Young St John the Baptist and Angels
72.4 × 54 cm, The Toledo Museum of Art, Toledo (Ohio). Gift of Edward Drummond Libbey

This *Virgin and Child* is an autograph example of Pesellino's work and has been described as 'one of the most sensuous devotional panels of the Renaissance'. Not surprisingly, several of Pesellino's compositions, including this panel, were imitated by followers of varying talent. The influence of Filippo Lippi is detectable in the composition, but the overlapping of the figures belies a close examination of contemporary sculpture, such as the reliefs of Luca della Robbia. The viewer's eye charts the recession into space from the parapet in the foreground, by way of the back of the throne in the middle distance, to the rose hedge behind, glimpsed through the wings of the angels and the looped curtains. This highly sophisticated spatial organization is also found in the paintings of *The Virgin and Child* by his slightly older contemporaries, Domenico Veneziano and Andrea del Castagno. There are breathtaking passages in this painting — the kerchief worn by the Virgin, the foreshortening of her right arm, or the drapery extending downwards from her left arm. The vitality comes from the characterization of the figures and the sharp light defining their forms.

61

JAN VAN EYCK (active 1422–1441)
The Madonna at the Fountain
19 × 12.5 cm, Koninklijk Museum voor Schone Kunsten, Antwerp

This unusually small devotional panel was painted late in the artist's life (1439) for private worship. The Virgin stands holding the Christ Child before a richly embroidered cloth of honour held by two angels. On the left is a brass fountain; behind is a low, fixed, brick bench placed in front of an enclosed rosegarden. The Child holds a string of coral beads. There are many layers of meaning within this composition, for the rosegarden and fountain were images of the Virgin. Van Eyck has here endeavoured to arrive at a definitive image concerning the role of the Virgin Mary in medieval Christian thought. As one writer has summarized it, 'In his final version of the Madonna, then, we find Jan creating a Virgin Mother whose incarnate son springs from her embrace in the same manner as the water of life springs from the fountain of gardens.' The viewer is shown that the Virgin and Child are the source of grace and divine life synonymous with the paradise evoked by the rosegarden. The small dimensions, simplified composition, and abundance of naturalistic representation give this picture a highly personal flavour. Panofsky wrote 'To look at it is an experience analogous to hearing a musical performance on the clavichord, where the ear, once adjusted to the small volume of the instrument, perceives dynamic differences more acutely than when exposed to more powerful sounds.'

62

JAN VAN EYCK (active 1422–1441)
The Virgin in a Church
31 × 14 cm, Gemäldegalerie, Staatliche Museen Preussischer Kulturbesitz, Berlin

The picture exhibits a technical mastery that epitomises early Flemish painting. Jan van Eyck was exceptional in his skill at observing and recording scenes in a style of such precision and accuracy that his images almost transcend reality. In this painting the eye is readily absorbed by the detailed treatment of architecture and light before sensing that the Virgin and Child seem disproportionately large in relation to the building. It would appear also after closer analysis that the sun enters the church through north-facing windows while at the same time a different source of light illuminates the Virgin and Child. Such distortion was clearly intended by van Eyck as a means of heightening the symbolism in the picture. The Virgin and Child stand alone in the nave of the church: the only other figures are angels glimpsed in the choir. The painter's purpose was not so much to paint the Virgin and Child in a church in any strictly physical sense, but rather to portray them as a personification of the spiritual force expressed architecturally by the church. Similarly, the fact that the treatment of light defies the laws of nature reveals van Eyck's intention to demonstrate the superiority of supernatural light over natural light. Such symbolism can be underpinned by quotations from scriptural texts. The Virgin is seen here not simply as the mother of Christ, but as the Church itself.

63

FOLLOWER OF ROBERT CAMPIN (1370/9–1444)
The Virgin and Child with Saints in an Enclosed Garden
119.9 × 148.8 cm, National Gallery of Art, Washington D.C.: the Samuel H. Kress Collection

Robert Campin was the leading painter in the Netherlands before Jan van Eyck. He worked in Tournai, where Rogier van der Weyden became his pupil. The artist has shown the Virgin and Child in a garden enclosed by a wall on three sides and a building on the fourth. The principal figures are joined by four saints: Catherine of Alexandria and John the Baptist to the left, and Barbara and Anthony Abbot to the right. The attributes held by these saints, and the location in an enclosed garden with an abundance of symbolic flowers, all indicate the devotional and mystical purpose of this large altarpiece. Thematically and compositionally the panel combines the Italian *sacra conversazione* with the North European depiction of the Paradise garden. The overall subject of the altarpiece appears to be the Redemption, in so far as the Christ Child reaches for the apple being proffered by St Barbara, and all the symbolism of the rest of the altarpiece underscores this main action. The painting, which came from an unidentified church in Bruges, is surrounded by its original frame and has an inscription referring to the Virgin as the Queen of Heaven. Campin's work has been the subject of much discussion in the recent past because of a whole group of paintings attributed to the so-called Master of Flémalle, whose exact identification within Campin's workshop is still being defined. Campin himself pioneered a style that moved away from the decorative international Gothic style and fused elements of Italian art and Franco-Burgundian sculpture to achieve greater realism.

64

STEPHAN LOCHNER (active 1442–1451)
The Virgin and Child with Angels in the Rosegarden
51 × 40 cm, Wallraf-Richartz-Museum, Cologne

The enclosed garden is a symbol of the Virgin's purity, and for similar reasons the rose too is a flower particularly associated with her. The garden could also represent Paradise, as surely it does here. Lochner depicts the crowned Virgin seated on a low bench. Behind her is a trellis, above which is God the Father. Angels surround the Virgin; some play musical instruments, and the two in the upper corners hold back a curtain that makes this wonderful image seem like a vision. The theme was much favoured by north European artists and this example by Lochner is one of the finest. Colour and drawing impress the picture on the mind. Few can resist the touching simplicity of the Virgin or the impish innocence of the angels. Lochner was born on the shores of Lake Constance, but he became the head of the school of painting in Cologne, combining the international Gothic style with a new sense of realism. Dürer admired his work.

65

JAN VAN EYCK (active 1422–1441)
The Virgin and Child with Saints and a Donor
47.3 × 61.3 cm, The Frick Collection, New York

Documentary evidence proves that this altarpiece was painted for the Carthusian monastery of Genadedal near Bruges for the prior, Jan Vos, and dedicated in 1443. It must, however, have been commissioned at least two years earlier, during the time of Jan Vos's predecessor as prior, because it is clear that Jan van Eyck himself could have worked on the altarpiece for only a few months before his own death in the summer of 1441. Subsequently Jan Vos became prior of the monastery at Nieuwlicht near Utrecht which was destroyed during the religious wars of the sixteenth century. Somehow the altarpiece survived, although it was not recorded again until the nineteenth century. The two female saints are St Barbara (on the left) and St Elizabeth of Hungary (on the right). St Barbara intercedes with the Virgin and Child on behalf of the donor, Jan Vos, who wears a Carthusian habit. The landscape behind the main figures extends from rural scenery on the left to a townscape on the right. Swans glide on the river and the local inhabitants go about their business totally oblivious of the more formal scene in the foreground. The town has not been identified, although it is painted with jewel-like delicacy in an intense light.

66

ROGIER VAN DER WEYDEN (c.1400–1464)
St Luke Painting the Virgin
135.3 × 108.8 cm, Museum of Fine Arts, Boston. Gift of Mr & Mrs Henry Lee Higginson

The legend that St Luke painted the Virgin was imported, most probably from the eastern Mediterranean, at an uncertain date and became established in Western Europe by the early Middle Ages. The subject was painted on several occasions by Flemish artists and remained popular in Northern Europe into the sixteenth century. This particular association meant that St Luke became the patron saint of painters, adding to his similar role for physicians and surgeons (which in one sense is more appropriate, for Luke was himself a medical man). Over the centuries there has also been an attempt to identify any pictures that St Luke actually painted, but such searches have proved to be fruitless. St Luke was in fact a Greek, the author of the gospel that dwelt at greatest length on the early life of Christ and that therefore served as one of the principal literary sources for religious artists. Rogier van der Weyden shows St Luke painting the Virgin while she feeds the Christ Child. A small carving depicting the Fall of Man decorates the arm of the Virgin's throne. An ox, the attribute of St Luke, can be made out in the small room on the right. This scene is located in an interior beyond which is a wall with two figures overlooking a townscape with a river. These two figures (sometimes identified as Joachim and Anna) are a marvellous visual conceit because, unlike the spectator whose pose and activity they emulate, they are unaware of the portentous event taking place in the foreground of the picture. Rogier van der Weyden's neat and meticulous style allows him to paint both an interior and a landscape with the greatest fidelity, particularly with regard to the different effects of light.

67
ROGIER VAN DER WEYDEN (c.1400–1464)
The Virgin and Child
100 × 52 cm, Museo del Prado, Madrid

The artist depicts the Virgin seated in a niche. She supports the Christ Child on her knee while he plays with — 'mutilates' would be a more accurate description — the pages of a book. The motif is derived from Jan van Eyck's *Virgin and Child* (the Ince Hall Madonna) now in Melbourne, but here Rogier van der Weyden reveals one of the main characteristics of his mature style (c.1438). He distances the viewer from the figure and concerns himself with mass and shape so that, in Panofsky's words, 'where Jan permits one to approach Our Lady in the familiar atmosphere of a domestic interior, however regally appointed, Rogier enjoins us, as it were, to kneel before a statue of the Queen of Heaven.' This emphasis on the sculptural is emphasized by making the figure seem like a piece of real sculpture, seated within an imagined niche; the plain background suggests an enclosed space, and in front is a projecting console. The decoration of the niche is kept very simple and the Virgin wears a simple kerchief as an angel hovers discreetly overhead with a crown. This is not so much 'a crown of glory as one of purity, perseverance and faith in sorrow'. The economy of Rogier van der Weyden's style in this picture even extends to the treatment of colour. For instance, 'instead of flowing and spreading like a cascade of liquid ruby, the robe of the Prado Madonna, its folds precise and, by comparison, sparse, seems to congeal into a concentrated plastic shape' (Panofsky). That, in sum, is the essence of Rogier van der Weyden's style.

68
ROGIER VAN DER WEYDEN (c.1400–1464)
The Virgin and Child Standing in a Niche
18.5 × 12 cm, Kunsthistorisches Museum, Vienna

It has been suggested that this small panel was the left wing of a diptych, the right wing of which (also in Vienna) shows *St Catherine in a Landscape*. Alternatively, both panels could once have belonged

together as two of the three parts of a triptych. The crowned Virgin stands suckling the Child in an imaginative niche painted in grisaille. At the top of the niche, above tracery, is God the Father and a dove; to the sides the Fall is represented. All these figures decorating the niche are rendered in a simulation of sculpture. The Virgin stands before a marble throne decorated with the lions of Solomon evidently intended to represent the *sedes sapientiae* and thus to symbolize the Virgin's wisdom. This panel is regarded as one of the earliest in Rogier van der Weyden's oeuvre, dating from the early 1430s. Both stylistically and iconographically it reveals the artist's debt to Jan van Eyck and Robert Campin. The small scale is unusual for Rogier van der Weyden, who favoured larger, more dramatically proportioned altarpieces.

69
DIERIC BOUTS (active 1457, died 1475)
The Virgin and Child
23 × 15 cm, National Gallery of Art, Washington D.C., Patron's Permanent Fund

Paintings of *The Virgin and Child* by Bouts oscillate between the ideal and the realistic. It is in the figure of the Virgin that the artist strives for the ideal, whereas the Christ Child is often depicted with disarming naturalness. The hands of the Virgin are particularly well observed. The viewer is conscious of the firm bone structure. The hair is drawn back behind the ear before falling downwards on to the shoulder. The forehead is prominent, the eyes narrow, the nostrils large, and the mouth full. All of these features are kept in place by the vertical axis extending from the parting in the hair, down the nose to the dimple in the chin. The rise and fall of the flesh is suggested by the play of light on the surface. The Virgin supports the Child with her hands. He seems more animated, with one hand on his stomach and the other tugging at the cloth on which he is seated. Panels of this type depicting half-length figures sometimes formed one half of a diptych, the other half often comprising a portrait. No doubt these works were meant for a domestic context so that the femininity of the Virgin and the more private aspects of her relationship with her son could be demonstrated.

70
WORKSHOP OF DIERIC BOUTS (1410/20–1475)
Virgin and Child
The Metropolitan Museum of Art, New York, Jack and Belle Linsky Collection

The quality of this painting is high, but it is not quite good enough to be attributed to Dieric Bouts himself whose style was close to that of Rogier van der Weyden. It has been described as the first surviving workshop copy of a lost painting by Bouts dating from his final years. The mood of the painting is distinctive. The figures both have smiling dispositions and the peaceful landscape is bathed in sun. The Christ Child inconsequentially plays with the toe of his right foot, but in his left hand he holds a single flower, a pink, which has spiked petals, prefiguring the nails that will be used to affix the grown Christ to the cross.

71
MASTER OF THE ST LUCY LEGEND (active 1480)
The Virgin and Child with SS. Catherine of Alexandria, Barbara, Ursula and Cecilia
79 × 60 cm, Detroit Institute of Arts

The painter was named by Friedländer after the altarpiece showing scenes from the life of St Lucy, painted in 1480 for the church of St Jacob, Bruges. The chief characteristics of his style are bright, decorative colouring and slender rather impassive female types with mask-like faces. There is some influence of Hans Memlinc, but it seems that the artist may have worked in Spain as well. Friedländer wrote, 'Three things distinguish the Master of the Legend of St Lucy — an understanding of architecture, intimate observation of the plant world, and a pleasing decorative sense.' The Virgin and Child are seated in a rosegarden attended by four female saints: 'a veritable gallery of young women of carefully varied types'. The painter has lavished a great deal of care particularly in depicting the draperies, headdresses and hair. Behind the garden, as though seen through a window, is a view of the city of Bruges, including the spire of Nôtre Dame and the belfry tower under construction — a view that is like a vignette and that was no doubt inspired to some extent by manuscript illumination. This artist nearly always included such a view of Bruges in his paintings.

72
HANS MEMLINC (active c.1465–1494)
The Virgin and Child
37.5 × 28 cm, National Gallery, London

The Virgin and Child are here depicted formally and with a fidelity that is comparable with Memlinc's portraiture. The composition shows that the artist was conversant with Italian representations of the theme, and it should be remembered that he was often employed by Italian patrons. The rather wooden handling of the Christ Child suggests participation by Memlinc's workshop; a date c.1475 has been suggested.

73
HANS MEMLINC (active c.1465–1494)
The Virgin and Child
44 × 33 cm, St John's Hospital, Bruges

The overall effect of this painting is one of opulence: it was clearly an important commission. The name of the patron, Martin Nieuwenhove, and the date (1487) are inscribed along the lower edge of the frame. Internal references to the patron are found in the coat-of-arms in the stained glass, and he is possibly the male figure reflected in the mirror at the left. The panel in fact formed the left wing of a diptych, the right wing of which is *A Portrait of Martin Nieuwenhove*. The whole of the painting of *The Virgin and Child* is full of reminiscences of Jan van Eyck: the rich brocade of the carpet and the cushion on the parapet, the precious stones on the Virgin's bodice, the diadem studded with pearls, the gold highlights on her hair, the mirror, the lighting of the interior, the view of a landscape through the half-open shutter on the left or the window on the right. Memlinc enriches the painting with sharply observed detail and faithfully records the different textures. The pyramidal shape of the Virgin and the type of the Christ Child are perhaps closer to Rogier van der Weyden. The artist shows the back view of the Virgin reflected in the mirror as though the donor in the role of the viewer is communicating directly with her. The overt search for formal beauty combined with the accumulation of detail somewhat negate the significance of the exchange of the apple between mother and son. It is a dignified composition of the highest quality.

74

GERARD DAVID (c.1460–1523)
The Virgin and Child
35 × 29 cm, Musées Royaux des Beaux-Arts, Brussels

The painting is memorable on account of its informality emphasizing the *genre*-like aspects of the theme of the Virgin and Child. The Virgin is shown feeding the Child now properly weaned. The painter has presented a purely domestic scene and taken particular care with the still-life objects. The furniture, food, utensils, book and basket are arranged or scattered around the room to create a feeling of intimacy. The view through the window, which is painted with characteristic precision, is shared with the Virgin by the viewer. As such, it is not only a compositional device, but a way of heightening the viewer's response to the subject. It is perhaps David's experience as a manuscript painter that allows him to carry off this unusual composition so successfully. Yet he was an artist who remained fixed within the fifteenth-century tradition. 'Slow-moving and barren of ideas, David's imagination failed to encompass growth. Creative only in picturing the enduring scene, he was neither epic nor dramatic. The events he shows have the effect of ceremonies, of symbolic acts. He shaped his looming, stratified masses like a sculptor, but placed them in the context of light and space like a painter. They are vessels of sentiment, these masses, not of the will.' (Friedländer).

75

GIOVANNI BELLINI (c.1430–1516)
The Virgin and Child
52 × 42.5 cm, Museo Correr e Quadreria Correr, Venice

Although this *Virgin and Child* is generally dated to the 1470s, it retains several stylistic features associated with Giovanni Bellini's early manner. There is a distinctly linear quality in the drawing and a certain hardness in the modelling of the draperies. Both these characteristics, however, are dominated by the feeling of human warmth and tenderness generated by the image of the Virgin keeping firmly hold of the Christ Child as he sits on the parapet. The viewer looks upwards at the figures, who are silhouetted against the sky: it is a device that at once concentrates the eye on the Virgin and Child and at the same time distances them from us. Bellini paradoxically succeeds in making the Virgin and Child seem to belong to two different worlds.

76

SANDRO BOTTICELLI (1445–1510)
The Virgin and Child
91 × 73 cm, Städelsches Kunstinstitut und Städtische Galerie, Frankfurt

The composition was frequently used by members of the Botticelli workshop: a number of versions exist. A date c.1490 is acceptable on the basis of the firm outline of the profiles and the clear delineation of the facial features. The figures are treated on a large scale, but even so the feeling of intimacy is by no means reduced: the Christ Child clings endearingly to his mother, and the young St John the Baptist looks on with a concerned expression.

77

GIOVANNI BELLINI (c.1430–1516)
The Virgin and Child with a Greek Inscription
82 × 62 cm, Pinacoteca di Brera, Milan

The Virgin and Child are seen from below, from a position coinciding, in fact, with the level of the parapet on which the Child stands. The proportions of the figures seem, therefore, to be monumental and the composition is notable for its imposing forms set against a simple background of a curtain suspended from a rail. The title of the picture is derived from the Greek letters in the upper corners referring to the Virgin and Child respectively. It is likely that a number of Bellini's renderings of this subject were painted for patrons with Greek or Eastern Orthodox Christian beliefs. Venice's contacts with the East had always been strong and its population was mixed. The formal treatment of the Virgin and Child in this picture also denotes the positive influence of Byzantine art on the painter. Indeed, the picture's quality is derived from the feeling of restraint, as well as from the exquisite drawing and modelling of the figures. The close harmony between the Virgin and Child is expressed not so much by the tenderness of the Virgin's embrace as by the fact that Bellini has placed their bodies on similar diagonals and made them look in the same direction. There is an overriding sense of pathos in the picture.

78

ANDREA MANTEGNA (1430/1–1506)
The Virgin and Child
43 × 32 cm, Gemäldegalerie Staatliche Museen Preussischer Kulturbesitz, Berlin

The worn appearance of the painting is due to the fact that Mantegna used canvas as the support and tempera for the medium. It was not unusual for him, in fact, to favour canvas over a panel. Suggested dates for this painting have varied enormously, but such matters are hardly relevant to an appreciation of such an arresting image of maternal love. The Christ Child is slumped in sleep while the Virgin cradles his head with her right hand and protects him by enveloping his small body within her mantle. The intimacy of the figures is perhaps only paralleled in the sculpture of Donatello, who worked in Padua between 1443 and 1454 and influenced Mantegna. Several of Donatello's compositions of *The Virgin and Child* were widely known at the time through plaquettes, but contact between the artists might have been direct, for Mantegna trained in Padua.

79

HANS MEMLINC (active c.1465–1494)
The Virgin and Child
24.8 cm (diameter), The Metropolitan Museum of Art, New York : the Friedsam Collection

Memlinc was a German by birth, but lived in Bruges where he painted many works for the international mercantile community in that city. He was trained in the workshop of Rogier van der Weyden, but adopted a softer, more pliant style, as displayed in this small roundel of the Virgin feeding the Christ Child: the landscape against which the figures are set seems to add to the informality of this intensely private work. Memlinc's art possesses the capacity to please: his immediate predecessors may have been pioneers, but Memlinc is generally more accessible. 'Jesus is not so much hero, champion, teacher and martyr as a beloved child, fussed over by gentle hands, or a loving and mourned son — in the narrow compass of the family rather than in cosmic grandeur. In Memlinc's devout vision, acceptance knew no struggle, dedication no doubts, no ecstatic crises. He saw the world of God in a state of Paradise, as an assemblage of pure beings, their bliss best exemplified in pleasing forms' (Friedländer).

80

HANS MEMLINC (active 1465–1494)
The Virgin and Child Enthroned with an Angel and a Donor
69 × 74 cm, Kunsthistorisches Museum, Vienna

The panel forms the centre of a triptych, with the figures of St John the Baptist (left) and St John the Evangelist (right) in the wings; the outside of the shutters was decorated with the figures of Adam and Eve. The altarpiece is in Memlinc's fully mature style and dates from c.1485. It demonstrates perfectly Friedländer's conception of the artist's devotional panels as being 'relaxed and without contrast. All opposites have lost their sharp edges — old and young, men and women, God and man, the blessed and the damned, rich and poor, good and evil. Even the executioners, the adversaries of Christ, share in the general air of youthful innocence and amiable activity.' The figures of the centre panel participate in this sense of well-being, and the setting exudes a similar mood through the rich brocades, the patterned carpet and a landscape that has the precision of engraved glass. Typical of Memlinc is the simulated sculpture (Abraham and Isaac on the left, and the Beheading of St Catherine on the right) at the top of the columns. These pieces of sculpture are interrupted, as it were, by the *putti* holding swags of fruit. If the *putti* should let go of the swags — a motif that Memlinc would have seen in Italian painting — the mood would be shattered.

81

CARLO CRIVELLI (1430/5–c.1500)
The Virgin and Child (Madonna della Candeletta)
218 × 75 cm, Pinacoteca di Brera, Milan

This tall and rather narrow panel once formed part of a large altarpiece painted c.1490 for the cathedral in Camerino. Although the artist often termed himself a Venetian citizen in the signatures on his paintings, he in fact worked for long periods in the Marches on the eastern seaboard of Italy. This panel of *The Virgin and Child* formed the centre of the altarpiece, flanked by whole-length figures of paired saints and topped by a scene of the Crucifixion. Altarpieces in the Marches were nearly always fitted with ornate gilt frames which were frequently decorated with further panels in the pilasters or in the predella. The main focus of such an altarpiece is the central axis, just as in this instance several of the many symbols shown in the main panel relate directly to the Crucifixion set immediately overhead. Crivelli has painted a particularly exotic rendering of *The Virgin and Child*. The viewer's eye is captivated by the representations of various fruits and flowers, as well as by the highly decorated brocades and the variety of veined marble. Added to this catalogue of still-life painting must be the vase containing the flowers and the single candle mysteriously attached to the marble step. It is from this candle that the painting derives its popular name. The pear, which is held by the Virgin, is a dual symbol of affection and well-being on account of the sweetness of its taste.

82
PIERO DELLA FRANCESCA (*c*.1416–1492)
Madonna della Misericordia
273 × 323 cm, Pinacoteca Comunale Borgo Sansepolcro

The panel is the central part of a polyptych commissioned for the chapel of the Company of the Misericordia in Borgo Sansepolcro in 1445. The artist was expected to finish the whole altarpiece in three years, but in fact the work took him fifteen years to complete. It was not only that the altarpiece comprised a large number of parts, but it was also that Piero della Francesca worked slowly. The columnar figure of the Virgin, her arms raised holding out her mantle, has a timeless quality enhanced by the high forehead, tall neck and the oval structure of the face. She might serve almost as a symbol of the Church. Most writers compare this noble figure with oriental or classical art. Whereas the Virgin appears as a universal figure, however, the figures sheltering at her feet are sharply observed as individuals, and there can be little doubt that they are likenesses of local people posed for the occasion. The crystalline light and the rich colouring of blue and red draperies make this one of the most moving images in Italian art.

83
ANDREA MANTEGNA (1430/1–1506)
The Virgin and Child
43 × 45 cm, Museo Poldi-Pezzoli, Milan

Like his painting of *The Virgin and Child* in Berlin, this too has been executed by Mantegna in tempera on canvas and possibly at a similar date (*c*.1485–95). The mood in both pictures is also comparable. Here the Virgin supports the Christ Child's sleeping head by the cheeks and appears to be winding him after a feed. The composition is essentially circular and the Child is contained within the Virgin's mantle. It is sometimes argued that the sleeping Christ Child anticipates the dead Christ of the Pietà, but this can hardly always be the case. Mantegna is surely appealing to broader human instincts, choosing perhaps to emphasize the Virgin's role as an intercessor for mankind in the guise of an ordinary mother. Such pictures evoke an equal response in viewers of all centuries.

84
MASTER OF THE MAGDALEN LEGEND
(*c*.1483–1527)
The Virgin and Child
26.5 × 18.4 cm, Musées Royaux des Beaux-Arts, Brussels

The Master of the Magdalen Legend in this picture consciously evokes comparison with the half-length Madonnas of Rogier van der Weyden in the search for purity of form by means of simplicity of design. The artist's personal characteristics, however, find expression and break the spell. This is most apparent in the contrived pose of the Christ Child as the Virgin supports the arm on which Christ rests His own sleeping head. The charm comes from the nonchalance with which this motif is introduced. The sleep represented here is that of an innocent peaceful child: it is surely not intended to prefigure the manner of Christ's death. The background of the panel has been decorated with punching, a pattern of decoration often used by the painter.

85
SANDRO BOTTICELLI (1445–1510)
The Madonna of the Magnificat
118 cm (diameter), Galleria degli Uffizi, Florence

The Virgin is shown in the act of composing the *Magnificat* (Luke 1: 46–55) while being crowned by two attendant angels. Significantly, the Virgin has inscribed the *Magnificat* as far as the beginning of the verse, 'For he that is mighty hath magnified me', while the Christ Child points to the word 'lowliness'. On this basis, it might be suggested that Botticelli has depicted a somewhat sophisticated and literary form of the Madonna dell' Umiltà. The composition is a masterly exercise in the arrangement of figures within a circular form. The two outer angels holding the crown provide an arch through which a landscape is seen. This is one of Botticelli's most famous paintings, dating from *c*.1485 when he was at the height of his powers. The clear outlines, firm drawing, and subtle modelling that so skilfully captures the rise and fall of human flesh are the essence of Botticelli's mature style.

86
SANDRO BOTTICELLI (1445–1510)
The Virgin and Child with a Book
58 × 39.5 cm, Museo Poldi-Pezzoli, Milan

The painting is on a small scale and has been brought to a high degree of finish by Botticelli. There is a clear connection with his painting of *The Madonna of the Magnificat* in the emphasis placed on the book, but this is a moment of greater intimacy between the Virgin and Child. The instruments of the Passion in the Child's right hand and the fruits displayed symbolically in the bowl imply that Christ's mission in this world is the topic of discussion between mother and child. The emphasis on the diagonal enables Botticelli to relate the figures to both the interior and to the forested landscape glimpsed through the window. Great attention has been paid to the painting of materials, such as the Virgin's veil and the cushion on which the book is placed, as well as to the depiction of the objects deposited randomly on the shelves. A date during the early 1480s is likely.

87
GIOVANNI BELLINI (*c*.1430–1516)
The Virgin and Child
88.9 × 71.1 cm, The Metropolitan Museum of Art, New York. The Rogers Fund

The idea of placing the seated Virgin behind a parapet is often found in Venetian paintings of the fifteenth century, but here the figures are also offset against a cloth of honour suspended over a rail. The Virgin and Child, therefore, are located in the middle distance, while behind them on the left is a landscape. The buildings are unmistakably Venetian, while the distant mountains are typical of northern Italy. The feeling of recession within the picture is achieved by a series of controlled 'steps' towards the background. Bellini has displayed his supreme sense of form in the modelling of the Virgin and Child (note particularly the foreshortening of the Child's limbs), at the same time demonstrating his continuing skill as a landscape painter. Such features suggest a date close to 1490. The Child holds a pear, a symbol of the Virgin.

88
GIOVANNI BELLINI (*c*.1430–1516)
The Madonna of the Pear
83 × 66 cm, Gallerie dell' Accademia Carrara, Bergamo

The painting is the best preserved of any of Giovanni Bellini's Madonnas, even though the blue of the Virgin's robe has deteriorated. The condition of the flesh tones is almost perfect, and therefore provides a valuable indication of the quality of Bellini's modelling. The artist has retained the usual props — the marble parapet in the foreground and the cloth of honour offsetting the figures — but these are not so prominent as to place too great an emphasis on the foreground. The Virgin and Child very subtly blend in with the landscape which has been described as 'a peopled view of almost Eyckian intensity'. The pear is a symbol of the Virgin because the sweetness of its juice is comparable with her character. The painting dates from *c*.1490 and is undoubtedly one of Bellini's masterpieces in which he has perfected beauty of form and feeling for landscape.

89
ATTRIBUTED TO TITIAN (TIZIANO VECELLIO)
(*c*.1477–1576)
Virgin and Child with SS. Anthony of Padua and Roch
92 × 133 cm, Museo del Prado, Madrid

This small *sacra conversazione* was recorded for the first time in Spain in 1657. It is a controversial painting that is sometimes attributed to Giorgione and more usually now to Titian. Both artists were trained in the workshop of Giovanni Bellini and both developed their own individual styles fairly rapidly, exercising a reciprocal influence on one another. This helps to explain why there are pronouncedly Giorgionesque features in the present painting, notably in the facial type of the Virgin (oval face and downcast eyes) and the physiognomy of the Christ Child, although the bold characterization of the saints and the broad handling of paint are more closely related to Titian (*c*.1510). The poses and expressions of the saints (St Anthony looking away from the Virgin and St Roch towards her) have a degree of animation that belies the style of Titian.

St Anthony of Padua was a Franciscan and his attribute is a lily: St Roch was a pilgrim who interceded on behalf of those afflicted with the plague. St Roch is often depicted by Venetian and Marchigian painters. The picture is unfinished, lacking the final layers of pigment on the Virgin's mantle, the landscape and part of St Anthony's habit. The most glorious part is the Virgin's red drapery, especially the gathering of the folds over the sleeve and on the step. The texture and colour are of the highest quality.

90

TITIAN (TIZIANO VECELLIO) (c.1477–1576)
The Virgin and Child (The Gipsy Madonna)
65.8 × 83.5 cm, Kunsthistorisches Museum, Vienna

The popular name of this picture, *The Gipsy Madonna*, stems from the dark hair and eyes of the Virgin. It is an early work by Titian (c.1510). The composition — the Child standing on a parapet and the Virgin placed in front of a sharply creased curtain, beyond which on the left is a mountainous landscape — relies upon Titian's master, Giovanni Bellini. Some influence of Titian's fellow pupil, Giorgione, can be detected in the elegiac mood of the landscape notable for the solitary figure seated below the tree. The deep colours, the neat tucks and folds in the drapery, and the sensuous modelling of the flesh are the basic ingredients of Titian's style that were to be dramatically developed in later decades.

91

ANONYMOUS, FERRARESE SCHOOL
The Virgin and Child with two Angels
58.5 × 44 cm, National Gallery of Scotland, Edinburgh

The painting dates from the late fifteenth century and is associated with the school of Ferrara. The most striking aspect is the *trompe l'oeil* effect of the torn canvas attached to the simulated stretcher of the picture. It is as though this has been deliberately broken in order to reveal the Virgin and Child: indeed, she seems to have released the Child — who is forced to hang on to her girdle for safety — so as to make the traditional gesture of welcome with her left hand. In her other hand she holds a pomegranate as a symbol of the Resurrection. She is seated on a low brick bridge on top of which two angels (with very pointed red shoes) approach. The effect is almost surreal and is one encountered more frequently in late fifteenth-century manuscripts produced in Padua and Venice. At the lower left corner of the painting in Edinburgh a fly can also be seen on a piece of the torn canvas. Other fifteenth-century painters, such as Carlo Crivelli, also included visual conceits of this type in their pictures. It seems that there is no moral or symbolic significance in the motif, and that it is really intended to display the painter's skill at still-life. Vasari, for instance, records the anecdote that Giotto could paint flies so convincingly that they looked real — an anecdote that had its origins in classical literature. It is likely that fifteenth-century painters wished to emulate this tradition and so win the admiration of their patrons.

92

VITTORE CARPACCIO (c.1460–1523/6)
The Virgin and Child Enthroned with Angels
138 × 171 cm, Scuola di San Giorgio degli Schiavoni, Venice

The painting is generally described as a late work (c.1520), and may have been carried out by an assistant following the master's design. The figure of the Virgin is conceived on a monumental scale, and there are only glimpses of landscape at the sides of the throne so that the eye does not escape all that easily into the background. The Virgin and Child are rather ponderous and heavy as types, and the contrast with the small dynamic angels is telling. The two angels at the top waft around on clouds carrying a crown between them, while below at the lower edge three more angels perform a dance, waving banderoles, on a parapet beneath the throne. These angels enliven the composition and lend it distinct charm: the Virgin and Child seem to ignore all such antics.

93

ALBRECHT DÜRER (1471–1528)
The Virgin and Child
24 × 18 cm, Kunsthistorisches Museum, Vienna

Dürer's narrative ability is perhaps most evident in his prints. His woodcuts portraying the *Life of the Virgin*, published in 1511, were deeply influential. He seems to have made fewer paintings than prints on the theme of the Virgin and Child. This picture, which is dated 1503, shows the Virgin feeding the Child. Such a homely subject reveals Dürer's great ability for capturing basic human qualities. He has chosen a robust peasant girl to represent the Virgin, who clearly enjoys carrying out the duties of motherhood. The large eyes, generous mouth and dimpled chin transmit a feeling of radiance that balances the Child's self-absorption in the act of feeding. There is a satisfying textural quality in the painting of the veil, but Dürer reserves his greatest effort for the spring-like coils of hair.

94

GIOVANNI BELLINI (c.1430–1516)
The Madonna of the Meadow
67 × 86 cm, National Gallery, London

The painting is widely acknowledged as one of the most perfect of all Bellini's creations. Dating from the first decade of the sixteenth century, the picture comes from that moment in the artist's working life when style and content are effortlessly blended. The Virgin and Child in the foreground dominate the composition; the pyramidal form of the Virgin's body is echoed by the hilltop town in the background and by the mountains seen in the further distance. The sleeping child is a clear reference to the theme of the Pietà, in which the Virgin cradles the body of her crucified Son, and much of the imagery in the painting underlines this connection — specifically the lion fighting a snake to the left of the Virgin, and the classical altar at the right edge. The most engaging aspect of the picture, however, is the pastoral emphasis in the setting that is not all that different from the rural flavour of Virgil's *Georgics*. The time of year is spring and people are tending the fields. There is a feeling of renewal and of regeneration most evident in the vegetation. Such a pastoral element in Bellini's work

had begun to make itself apparent during the 1470s, but not until the *Madonna of the Meadow* did the artist achieve that sense of the permeation of nature by the divine which is the essence of his late masterpieces.

95

NICHOLAS FROMENT (active 1461–1483)
The Virgin in the Burning Bush
410 × 305 cm, Saint Sauveur Cathedral, Aix-en-Provence

The Virgin in the Burning Bush is the centre panel of a large triptych with folding wings, commissioned by King René of Anjou in 1476 for a private chapel in the Carmelite church at Aix-en-Provence. In the left shutter King René of Anjou is shown being presented by SS. Mary Magdalen, Anthony and Maurice; in the right shutter Queen Jeanne de Laval is represented with SS. John the Evangelist, Catherine and Nicholas. The scene of the Annunciation painted in grisaille to resemble sculpture is shown on the outside of the shutters. Whereas the portraits in the wings of the altarpiece are important for their realism, the iconography of the centre panel is almost idiosyncratic and the image is clearly symbolic. The burning bush is a symbol of the Virgin that refers to her purity. The male figure in the lower right corner is Moses, to whom God appeared in a burning bush. This last is an event in the Old Testament that prefigures the Annunciation, and is here directly posited by the pose of the angel approaching Moses. The medallion worn by the angel depicts the Fall of Man, while the Christ Child holds a mirror in which is reflected the image of the Virgin and Child as a symbol of salvation. What is represented in this centre panel is in essence the virginity of Mary. The iconography is rarely found in painting and relates far more closely to manuscript tradition. Apart from his abilities as a portrait painter and as a deviser of symbolic images, Froment also reveals his skill as a landscapist with a splendid view into the far distance.

96

GIORGIONE (GIORGIO BARBARELLI) (c.1478–1510)
The Virgin and Child Enthroned
200 × 152 cm, Veneto Duomo, Castelfranco

Although of uncertain date, the altarpiece is widely acknowledged as a key work by Giorgione, executed for the painter's home town. It is a large work, with a simple yet imposing composition. The Virgin and Child are raised on a tall throne that extends the full height of the altarpiece and is positioned in the middle distance. On either side of the throne is a saint — St Francis to the right, and St Liberale to the left. In the background is a landscape clearly inspired by the countryside around Castelfranco. The coat-of-arms on the base of the throne is identifiable as that of the Costanzo family, who may have commissioned the altarpiece c.1505. Giorgione was a pupil of Giovanni Bellini, together with Titian. Only a few works can be attributed definitely to his hand, yet he played a major role in the development of European painting through his lyrical style and warm, glowing colours. The Castelfranco altarpiece has a meditative calm that is echoed in the peaceful landscape bathed in an evening light. The drawing of the figures and the modelling of the draperies are remarkably assured, just as the spatial intervals are of the greatest eloquence.

97

GIOVANNI BELLINI (c.1430–1516)
The Virgin and Child Enthroned
500 × 235 cm, San Zaccaria, Venice

The San Zaccaria altarpiece is dated 1505 and is one of the artist's finest paintings. It is still on the altar for which it was originally painted, surrounded by a marble frame. John Ruskin described it as one of the two best pictures in the world. The Virgin and Child are seated on a marble throne at the foot of which an angel plays a stringed instrument. The central figures are flanked by SS. Peter and Catherine to the left, and SS. Jerome and Lucy to the right. Each of these figures is absorbed in his or her own thoughts, thereby investing the painting with a contemplative calm. A sense of grandeur is derived from the imposing setting, which is the apse of a church, its vault decorated with simulated mosaics. The painted architecture gives the impression that the space inhabited by the figures is an extension of the real space in the church of San Zaccaria, a visual effect that is increased by a viewpoint almost on a level with the Virgin. This is one of the works in which Bellini comes to terms with the High Renaissance: the treatment of the architecture, the smooth modelling, the even distribution of the light, the soft modelling of the draperies, and the rich colouring are of superlative quality.

98

TITIAN (TIZIANO VECELLIO) (c.1477–1576)
The Virgin and Child (The Madonna of the Cherries)
81 × 99.5 cm, Kunsthistorisches Museum, Vienna

The composition of half-length figures grouped behind a parapet is still reminiscent of Giovanni Bellini, but the interpretation and technique show how rapidly Titian developed his style. Even within the space of five years the contemplative mood of *The Gipsy Madonna* has given way to a more sophisticated composition, a bolder use of colour and a broader range of brushwork. *The Madonna of the Cherries*, dating from c.1515, has a maturity and breadth that foreshadows some of Titian's subsequent achievements. The Virgin is placed before a backcloth on either side of which are Joseph (to the left) and Zacharias (to the right). The offspring of these two male figures provide a quickening of rhythm that counteracts the symmetrical arrangement of the main figure. The Christ Child leans towards the Virgin while the young St John the Baptist looks up from the lower right corner. The children, in fact, form a triangle with the Virgin, but this is done in a way that adds variety to the composition through the introduction of the motifs of the cherries. This symbol of the Passion has been handed to the Christ Child by St John the Baptist, and he shows the fruit to the Virgin. A similar motif can be found in a painting by Albrecht Dürer dated 1506 which may have been known to Titian, for the German painter visited Venice in that year.

99

SEBASTIANO DEL PIOMBO (c.1485–1547)
The Holy Family with St John the Baptist and a Donor
97.8 × 106.7 cm, National Gallery, London

Sebastiano del Piombo derived his name from his appointment as keeper of the papal seal (*piombo*) in 1531. He was, however, born in Venice, where he was trained by Giovanni Bellini and modelled his early style on Giorgione. After moving to Rome in 1511 he altered his style in accordance with the innovations of Raphael and particularly Michelangelo. Something of the duality in Sebastiano del Piombo's style is present in this painting of *The Holy Family* (c.1520). The horizontal format with three-quarters length figures is essentially Venetian, but the composition is more nearly related to painting styles of central Italy. The large forms ranging along diagonals and the expansive gestures create a dynamism that seems to be hardly contained within the picture space. This internal rhythm is maintained by the way in which all the figures, except for the Christ Child, avoid eye contact with the viewer. The Virgin and Child are vividly illuminated whereas other figures are seen only in half-light. The donor, carefully positioned beneath the Virgin's extended arm, might be identifiable with Pierfrancesco Borgherini, for whom Sebastiano worked in Rome on more than one occasion. It is possible that the basic idea of the composition was provided for Sebastiano del Piombo by Michelangelo, as happened in several other instances.

100

LEONARDO DA VINCI (1452–1519)
The Madonna with the Carnation
62 × 47.5 cm, Alte Pinakothek, Munich

The influence of Verrocchio is still apparent in this fairly early Virgin and Child by Leonardo da Vinci. The picture is normally dated c.1478, and is in many respects a highly traditional work. The figures are set in the foreground, the Christ Child seated on a cushion placed on a parapet. He reaches forward to touch the carnation (the Greek word for which means 'flower of God') held by the Virgin. Behind the figures is a spacious interior with two arched openings through which a mountainous landscape can be seen. The tall figure of the Virgin provides a compositional link between the foreground and background achieved by the fact that Leonardo locates her head on a line with the arches. The design, including the view through to the landscape and the vase of flowers in the lower right corner, contains features inspired by Verrocchio, but the treatment of light, the sudden changes of rhythm in the drapery, the importance given to gesture, and the character of the landscape with its massive mountain range are all intimations of Leonardo da Vinci's greatness. As Clark wrote, 'The Munich Madonna has the unpleasant vitality of immature genius.'

101

ANDREA VERROCCHIO (c.1435–1488)
The Virgin and Child
75.5 × 54.8 cm, Gemäldegalerie Staatliche Museen Preussischer Kulturbesitz, Berlin

Verrocchio was a distinguished sculptor as well as a painter, and his concern to bring a sense of volume

to two-dimensional forms can be observed in this early painting of *The Virgin and Child*. The Virgin is seated in three-quarters profile on a diagonal that is counteracted by another created by the Christ Child's body. The most important aspect of the picture, however, is the landscape, which is not treated simply as a backdrop but as a veritable space inhabited by the Virgin and Child. The contours of the hills and the rounded form of the promontory on the left are carefully integrated with the Virgin's body. It is as though the figures and the landscape have been made in a single mould. This was, of course, a facet of Verrocchio's art that his pupil Leonardo da Vinci was to make the foundation of his style. It was in a painting such as this that Verrocchio first took a composition often used by Florentine sculptors of the mid-fifteenth century and translated it into pictorial terms.

102

DOMENICO GHIRLANDAIO (1449–1494)
The Virgin and Child
73.4 × 50.8 cm, National Gallery of Art, Washington D.C.: the Samuel H. Kress Collection

A profound formative influence on Ghirlandaio was the work of Verrocchio, in whose workshop he was most probably trained. This *Virgin and Child* is one of Ghirlandaio's earliest works and demonstrates his close connection with Verrocchio, especially in the decorative features such as the Virgin's headdress and oval brooch, as well as the striped sash around the Christ Child's waist. There is also a distinctly sculptural feel that reveals a further debt to Verrocchio: the Virgin's body seems to swell to fill the lower part of the panel, and the Child's hair is worked as if it is in marble. Yet Ghirlandaio's own stylistic traits are already apparent in the calmer, more descriptive depiction of the facial features and the hands, where light plays a very positive role in the suggestion of the rise and fall of flesh. The gold background is somewhat of an anachronism for a picture of this date (c.1470) and may have been a later adjustment.

103

PIETRO PERUGINO (c.1445–1523)
The Virgin and Child
70.2 × 50.8 cm, National Gallery of Art, Washington D.C.: the Samuel H. Kress Collection

Vasari, in his *Life of Perugino*, described the artist as 'not a religious man, and would never believe in the immortality of the soul, obstinately refusing to listen to all good reasons'. Strangely, regardless of this evidence, Perugino produced some of the most moving religious images in Italian art. This *Virgin and Child*, painted c.1500, is typical of his treatment of the theme. The figures fill the foreground and are silhouetted against a peaceful landscape that complements the Virgin's pensive expression. The massive form of the Virgin seems to be absorbed in her own thoughts while the Christ Child is distracted by something beyond the picture space. Perugino painted many such panels and had several Umbrian imitators.

104
RAPHAEL (RAFFAELLO SANZIO) (1483–1520)
The Virgin and Child with the Young St John the Baptist and another Child (The Terranuova Madonna)
86 cm (diameter), Gemäldegalerie Staatliche Museen Preussischer Kulturbesitz, Berlin

After Raphael travelled from Umbria to Florence in 1504, he came under the influence of fresh and powerful influences such as Leonardo da Vinci and Michelangelo. In paintings like the Terranuova Madonna (so named after a previous owner) one observes Raphael adjusting his Umbrian-based style in order to incorporate motifs that he would have seen in works by Leonardo da Vinci. The foreshortening of the Virgin's left hand, the expression on her face, the twisting pose of the Christ Child and the relationship of the Virgin's body to the landscape display knowledge of Leonardo, especially of his *Madonna with the Yarnwinder* of 1501. Where Raphael falters is in trapping the figures in the foreground in front of a wall that bisects the composition horizontally and in his failure to relate the two other children to the Virgin and Child convincingly. These were matters that would be put right within a few years in paintings like *The Madonna of the Meadow* (Vienna) or the *Belle Jardinière* (Paris).

105
RAPHAEL (RAFFAELLO SANZIO) (1483–1520)
The Virgin and Child (The Large Cowper Madonna)
80.7 × 57.5 cm, National Gallery of Art, Washington D.C.; the Andrew W. Mellon Collection

The Large Cowper Madonna is dated 1508. It may have been executed just after Raphael reached Rome and then been sent back to Florence. At the close of the eighteenth century this painting and another smaller one of the same subject by Raphael were in the collection of the third Earl Cowper: both paintings are now in the National Gallery of Art, Washington, and are referred to respectively as the Large and Small Cowper Madonnas. The composition of the Large Cowper Madonna is ebullient, and the figures are conceived on a monumental scale. The series of the Madonna pictures that Raphael undertook in Florence represents in essence a process of assimilation, but in this example it is as though he suddenly breaks free. The artist had experimented on numerous occasions with the pose of the Child sprawling in the Virgin's lap, and had often shown him tugging at his mother's dress, but none of the solutions so far produced had quite the same degree of confidence as the Large Cowper Madonna. The rapport between the two figures, the freedom in the handling of the Virgin's fluttering drapery (especially the veil and the sleeve), the subtle colouring, the gentle modulation of flesh tones, and the silhouetting of the figures against a luminous sky reveal Raphael on the threshold of his masterpieces in Rome. The painting seems remarkably spontaneous but was, in fact, the result of reflection and distillation. Raphael here is the equal of Leonardo da Vinci.

106
FRANCESCO FRANCIA (active 1482–1517)
The Virgin and Child
61 × 46 cm, The Metropolitan Museum of Art, New York. Gift of Lewis C. Ledyard III, Mrs Victor Onet and Mrs T. F. Turner, in memory of Lewis C. Ledyard

Francia began his career as a goldsmith, and was often employed in that capacity at the courts of Ferrara and Bologna. He is first recorded as a painter in 1486, but he frequently referred to himself as a goldsmith in the signatures to his paintings. Francia's artistic origins explain the careful finish and meticulous technique of his pictures. This *Virgin and Child* is remarkably well-preserved, so that Francia's technical skills are immediately apparent. Although he was at first influenced by Ferrarese artists, after 1500 he became increasingly attracted to the example of Umbrian painting, particularly Perugino. Here the Virgin and Child, as in Perugino's work, are placed before a peaceful landscape that sets the mood of the picture. The pose of the Christ Child, however, to some extent counteracts this feeling of solemnity: he tugs at his mother's mantle and rests one foot on top of the other. Francia ran a large workshop and his compositions were often duplicated, but this is an autograph example of the highest quality and is in superb condition.

107
FRANCIABIGIO (FRANCESCO DI CRISTOFANO) (c.1482–1525)
The Virgin and Child
90 × 70 cm, Pinacoteca Nazionale, Bologna

Franciabigio collaborated with Andrea del Sarto, whose influence is apparent in this shrewdly devised composition of *The Virgin and Child* (c.1520). The artist carefully blends the figures together to make a single outline silhouetted against the landscape. The three-quarters length figure of the Virgin supporting the Christ Child looms large in the foreground, and the viewer is conscious of the solidity of this grouping. Yet this feeling of plasticity is reduced by the fusion of the figures with the landscape, the *sfumato* modelling and the warm tone. Freedberg described Franciabigio's picture in effective (although rather tortured) prose as follows: 'The figures still act ponderously, but their relation in movement is far more responsively calculated than before: the two shapes of the Madonna and Child confront each other in an interlocking pattern of parallel rhythms, not of isolated repetitions . . . This picture makes a unity of impressive, even rather grand form, heavily and still rather awkwardly movemented; and this quality of form is that also of its human content — a grave pathos, all the more convincing for the touch of awkwardness with which it is expressed.'

108
LUCAS CRANACH THE ELDER (1472–1553)
The Virgin and Child
71.1 × 52.1 cm, National Gallery of Art, Washington D.C. Gift of Adolf Caspar Miller

Cranach established a high viewing point for this picture so that the spectator looks slightly down at the Virgin and Child, and even more steeply down on the parapet. Although the artist was conscious of

Italian High Renaissance art, and on occasions demonstrated his knowledge of works by Leonardo da Vinci and Raphael, he retained a highly individual flavour in his paintings exemplified best perhaps in his treatment of the female nude and his memorable portraits. This picture of *The Virgin and Child*, painted c.1535, is not far removed from *genre* painting in its degree of informality. The Virgin, for example, seems to be trying very hard to interest the Christ Child in the fruit and drink she proffers him, but he appears to be equally reluctant to stand still, and instead looks out at the spectator. If anything, this device enhances the significance of the symbolism in that the suggestion is that, although the viewer may understand these references to Christ's future role, the Child himself chooses to ignore them. It is characteristic of German painters to depict the Virgin wearing such sumptuous garments.

109
HANS BALDUNG GRIEN (1484/5–1545)
The Virgin and Child with an Angel
91 × 64 cm, Gemäldegalerie Staatliche Museen Preussischer Kulturbesitz, Berlin

The Virgin appears here as an unusually sensual figure. The hair tumbles over her shoulders, she wears both a pendant and a diadem, and the drapery has a velvet sheen. Interestingly, the subject of the painting was once thought to depict Charity, but there are too many references to Christ's Passion for such an interpretation to be acceptable. The Child, for example, has fallen asleep in a manner that foreshadows his death and anticipates the scene of the Pietà. The figure behind the Virgin is an angel holding a bunch of grapes that symbolizes Christ's blood and the sacrament of the wine. The painting was probably painted towards the end of the 1530s. Baldung was a pupil of Dürer: he worked mainly in Strasbourg, which was a leading centre of the Reformation in Germany.

110
GERARD DAVID (c.1460–1523)
Virgin and Child with Angels
The Metropolitan Museum of Art, New York
Gift of Mr and Mrs Charles Wrightsman

In many ways David is the culmination of the Bruges school of painting where he worked in the tradition of van Eyck, Rogier van der Weyden, Memlinc and Hugo van der Goes. This accounts for his neat meticulous style, which is allied to his output as a miniaturist, but on the whole he remained a retardataire figure in early Netherlandish art. Many of his compositions were dependent on those of his predecessors. Friedländer wrote of David, 'Creative only in picturing the enduring scene, he was neither epic nor dramatic. The events he shows have the effect of ceremonies, of symbolic acts. He shaped his looming, stratified masses like a sculptor, but placed them in the context of light and space like a painter. They are vessels of sentiment, these masses, not of the will.' Such words are applicable here where the standing Virgin shown within a Gothic edifice and the closely observed landscape recall van Eyck. The four angels, however, so symmetrically placed and tending more towards pattern, are closer to Rogier van der Weyden in feeling. David's tendency to emulate earlier masters should in no way detract from his ability as a painter.

111

BERNAERT VAN ORLEY (c.1492–1541/2)
The Virgin and Child with Angels by a Fountain
85.4 × 69.9 cm, The Metropolitan Museum of Art,
New York. Bequest of Benjamin Altman

Van Orley worked mainly in Brussels, and in
addition to being a painter he made numerous
cartoons for stained glass and tapestries. His narrative
style is strong, and he absorbed a great deal from the
artists of the Italian High Renaissance, especially
Raphael. A feature of many of his paintings is the
inclusion of elaborate buildings, often in a variety of
architectural styles and clearly imaginary. Such a
building occurs in the right background of this
Virgin and Child, which dates from c.1513. The
Virgin is seated with the Child in a garden. Two
angels sing lustily, following the music in a song-
book: two birds (one a peacock) are perched on the
wall behind the Virgin. Prominent on the left is an
ornamental fountain. As a source of water, the
fountain represents spiritual life and salvation. When
associated with the Virgin Mary the fountain is an
allusion to the Immaculate Conception. The
peacock symbolizes immortality. Van Orley places
the scene in a landscape dominated by a village on a
hilltop. A man walks a dog along the road going
towards the village unaware of the vision of heaven.

112

ANDREA DEL SARTO (1486–1530)
The Madonna of the Harpies
208 × 178 cm, Galleria degli Uffizi, Florence

The altarpiece, dating from 1517, derives its name
from the figures of harpies painted in simulation of
sculpture as decoration on the base of the pedestal on
which the Virgin stands. Their role in the altarpiece
is made clear by the inscription from an obscure
fourteenth-century hymn celebrating the
Assumption of the Virgin. Harpies are of course
derived from antique art, but by the time of the
Renaissance they were associated with the translation
of the soul from the earthly to the heavenly sphere.
The altarpiece was painted for the church now
known as San Francesco de' Macci in Florence.
Stylistically it is one of the most notable
achievements of the High Renaissance, emulating
works by Raphael and Fra Bartolommeo. The artist
fuses the different parts of the composition together to
make a single unit, an effect achieved not only by the
gracefully interrelated poses of the figures, but also by
the modulation of colour. The subtle integration of
the two flanking saints (Francis and John the
Evangelist) with the strong central axis formed by
the Virgin and Child raised on the pedestal is an
able demonstration of the classical qualities of High
Renaissance art.

113

BUGIARDINI (1475–1554)
*The Virgin and Child with SS. Mary Magdalen and John
the Baptist*
194.3 × 165.6 cm, The Metropolitan Museum of
Art, New York. Fletcher Fund

This small altarpiece was originally in the church of
Santa Maria Maddelena all' Isola, Incise Valdarno
(Tuscany), and was possibly painted for a member
of the Altoviti family. It was for many years
attributed to Fra Bartolommeo, by whom
Bugiardini was influenced. In many ways the

painting is a superb summary of developments in
Florentine painting after Raphael departed for Rome
(1508). The unified composition, the fluid
movements and the accuracy of the modelling and
drawing reveal a considerable debt to Raphael, but
Bugiardini also introduces several personal touches:
St Mary Magdalen offers her pot of ointment to the
Virgin, the Christ Child sits cross-legged, and there
is a sprig in St John the Baptist's cross. The well-
nigh perfect condition of the picture allows one to
admire the vivid colouring and also to see the
changes made by the artist to his original design
(observe the alterations to the profile of St Mary
Magdalen and the right arm of St John the Baptist).
A date of 1510–15 is accepted.

114

ANDREA DEL SARTO (1486–1530)
Head of the Madonna (fragment)
38.1 × 29.2 cm, The Metropolitan Museum of Art,
New York. Bequest of Michael Friedsam: the
Friedsam Collection

The panel has been cut down from a larger painting
of *The Virgin and Child with the Young St John the
Baptist* known from a seventeenth-century engraving.
The composition is clearly inspired by one of
Raphael's famous Florentine Madonnas, such as the
Madonna del Cardellino (c.1506), and was no doubt
undertaken fairly early in Andrea del Sarto's life
while he was still influenced by his master, Piero di
Cosimo. The style of this fragment is thus a good
example of the artist's work before he began to use
the methods of Leonardo da Vinci. Even so,
Andrea del Sarto's soft, caressing brushwork and
delicate modelling of the flesh tones are readily
apparent in this sensitive image of the Virgin.

115

ANTONIO ALLEGRI CORREGGIO (c.1494–1534)
The Virgin and Child with the Young St John the Baptist
64.2 × 50.4 cm, The Art Institute of Chicago.
Clyde M. Carr Fund

The Virgin is seated on a grassy bank in front of a
trellis of lemon trees beyond which, on the right, is a
mountainous landscape. The Child blesses the
young St John the Baptist. The formal relationship
between the figures and the setting is extremely
subtle. The Virgin's legs, for instance, are directed
towards the right, but she twists herself round so that
the upper part of her body faces left. The artist
cleverly exploits the diagonals established by this
pose, and in so doing reflects the influences of
Leonardo da Vinci (also apparent in the Virgin's
face) and Raphael. The painting is a fairly early
work (c.1515), but already imparts something of
Correggio's seductive modelling of flesh and feeling
for landscape, aspects of his style that won him a
major reputation as leader of the Emilian School.

116

ANTONIO ALLEGRI CORREGGIO (c.1494–1534)
The Madonna of the Basket
33 × 25 cm, National Gallery, London

The small scale of this picture, which dates from the
mid-1520s, is matched by the intimacy of the scene.
Joseph is located in the right-hand background,
plying his trade as a carpenter, while the Virgin
appears to have been busy mending clothes, judging

from the basket and scissors in the lower left corner.
These subsidiary elements in the picture create the
atmosphere in which the Virgin gently restrains the
Christ Child, attempting to dress him while he
writhes and wriggles on her knee. The emphasis on
maternal love is also apparent in the pose of the
Virgin as she enfolds the Christ Child within her
arms. Only his head in fact breaks the beautifully
soft, rounded forms of her body. Correggio's
inspiration for this totally captivating composition
was most probably sculpture. It is amazing,
however, to what extent the artist's harmonizing of
colours, treatment of draperies, and ability to relate
figures and background anticipate French
eighteenth-century painting. Like many of
Correggio's pictures, *The Madonna of the Basket* was
widely copied and often engraved.

117

AGNOLO BRONZINO (1503–1572)
*The Holy Family with St Anne and the young St John
the Baptist*
124.5 × 99.5 cm, Kunsthistorisches Museum,
Vienna

This picture is a supreme demonstration of the art of
Mannerism by one of the main exponents of that
refined style in Florence. The composition (c.1550) is
one of pure artifice in so far as it deliberately eschews
any sense of spatial rationality. The Christ Child
and the young St John the Baptist are perceived on
rock ledges behind which the trio comprising St
Anne, the Virgin and Joseph is positioned. Beyond
them stretches a landscape dominated by a dark and
threatening sky that bathes the buildings in a lurid
light. By contrast, the lighting of the foreground is
totally artificial. Similarly, the complicated turning
poses of the main figures are meant to be admired for
the skilful drawing and placement. Both the holy
children, for example, are deliberately 'posed' in the
same way as people 'pose' for the camera today. Yet
this is not a totally cerebral painting, for the
contrapposto of the Virgin's body suggests a
quickening of rhythm that can be interpreted as an
expression of maternal concern. The careful
delineation and the smooth modelling that gives the
flesh a metallic lustre are also the chief features of
Bronzino's drawings. Freedberg describes this
picture as exhibiting 'a new suavity and breadth of
form . . . mingled with a delicate sobriety of feeling'.

118

JAN GOSSAERT (1475/8–1532)
The Virgin and Child
Koninklijk Museum voor Schone Kunsten, Antwerp

The dominant feature in the painting is the elaborate
marble throne on which the Virgin is seated, which
bears no spatial relationship with the landscape that
stretches behind into the far distance. The viewer is
given only a slightly raised viewpoint for the figures,
but the eye then looks steeply downwards on to the
landscape. The throne itself is a figment of the artist's
imagination and lacks all architectural logic. In
some respects, particularly the ornamentation, it is
pseudo-classical architecture of the type that
Netherlandish artists often introduced into their
paintings. Such artifice was one of the features of
northern Mannerist art. The dove representing the
Holy Ghost is positioned immediately above the
Virgin and Child.

119

HANS HOLBEIN THE YOUNGER (1496/7–1543)
The Virgin and Child with Members of the Meyer Family
146.5 × 102 cm, Schlossmuseum, Darmstadt

The picture is often referred to as the 'Meyer Madonna' or the 'Darmstadt Madonna', and has been described as 'the most famous, the last, and probably the greatest of Holbein's altarpieces' (Rowlands). Such pivotal significance can be attached to the altarpiece because it is not only Holbein's finest religious work, but it also contains some of his best portraits. The painting was most probably begun in 1526, but altered in 1528 after Holbein returned from his first visit to England, at which time he began to concentrate more on portrait painting. The iconography of the Madonna della Misericordia is cleverly used by Holbein as the central motif of the altarpiece. The Virgin shelters members of the Meyer family beneath her extended cloak. Joseph Meyer, a former Burgomaster of Basle, is on the left. Opposite him and nearest to the Virgin on the right is Meyer's first wife, Magdalena Baer, who had died at least fifteen years earlier, in 1511: this portrait was added in 1528. Meyer's second wife, Dorothea Kannengiesser (whom he had married in 1513), is next in the group on the right. In front of Meyer are his two sons who died before reaching manhood. The only surviving child of his second marriage was Anna, who kneels with her mother in the right foreground. Holbein made a series of distinguished drawings of the Meyer family in preparation for the picture. The relationship between Holbein and the Meyer family was a close one. Jacob Meyer had commissioned important works from Holbein that helped to establish the artist's reputation. Unfortunately, Meyer fell from power in 1521 and was accused of corruption. He also upheld the traditional Catholic religion in the face of the growing demand for reform within the city of Basle. On all these accounts, therefore, this private altarpiece painted for Jacob Meyer has an added poignancy.

120

JAN GOSSAERT (1475/8–1532)
The Virgin and Child
47.7 × 38.2 cm, Gemäldegalerie Staatliche Museen Preussischer Kulturbesitz, Berlin

Gossaert was a prominent court artist who worked in Antwerp, Middleburg and Breda. A visit to Rome in 1508/9 deeply influenced his style, which was nurtured on the legacy of van Eyck and further inspired by Dürer and artists of the Italian Renaissance. The Virgin has been feeding the Child, who reclines on a marble parapet. His attention is taken up with the bunch of grapes in the Virgin's left hand while he holds an apple in his right hand. The figures are set before an illusionistically painted marble slab bounded by a frame inscribed in Latin 'A true man and God, a pure mother and virgin'. Gossaert, who painted several pictures based on classical mythology, has depicted a rather becoming Virgin, elegantly attired with her hair flowing down over the shoulders. The chiaroscuro lighting adds to the feeling of underlying sensuality. Several paintings by Gossaert from his late phase (c.1530) employ the device of a marble frame behind the figures. It is possible that the panel formed part of a diptych or triptych.

121

JOOS VAN CLEVE (c.1464–1540)
The Virgin and Child
73.5 × 54.5 cm, The Metropolitan Museum of Art, New York: the Jack and Belle Linsky Collection

The composition (c.1525) is a marvellous fusion of figure painting, landscape and still-life. There is hardly any part of the surface that does not beguile the eye. The landscape has all the sense of poetry and concern for detail that is found in works by Patinir. The figures are silhouetted against this distant view that forms such a contrast with the finesse of the objects placed on the parapet in the immediate foreground — a bowl of fruit, a nut, a knife, half a lemon, a glass beaker. These subjects are arranged in a way that foreshadows a Dutch seventeenth-century still-life painting and, as in many of those pictures, an allegorical interpretation is intended. Here, of course, the references are to Christ's Passion. This exercise in still-life is extended to include the Book of Hours on the Virgin's lap, and the different textures of her draperies. As regards figure painting, the forms of the Virgin and Child are perfectly moulded to evoke a unified image that reflects knowledge of Leonardo da Vinci or Raphael. The Christ Child, having been breast-fed, is satiated and has fallen asleep. He holds the apple symbolizing the Fall of Man and wears a coral necklace traditionally believed to possess the power to ward off evil.

122

QUINTEN MASSYS (1465/6–1530)
The Virgin Standing with Angels
54.5 × 37.5 cm, Musée des Beaux-Arts, Lyons

The visual tradition for this type of *Virgin and Child* stretches back to Robert Campin and Jan van Eyck. Although at first Massys seems to evoke the ambience of a church, the building is open to the landscape at the back and resembles more closely a palace. It is likely that in this devotional panel (c.1510) the artist has endeavoured to create a metaphorical image whereby the Virgin and Child are the embodiment of the new church. Beyond the archway, and only partly represented, is an elaborate throne ultimately to be occupied by the Virgin and her Son. Similarly, the Old Testament figures that can be made out as simulated sculpture within the arch testify to the status of the Virgin as the fulfilment of biblical prophecy. The painting is therefore an example in a well-established Netherlandish tradition, but to heighten its impact Massys has introduced Italianate motifs like the swags of fruit, the reference to classical architecture and grotesques, and the gambolling *putti*. What Massys achieves is in effect an updated icon. His types depend in some respects upon Leonardo da Vinci, with the result that the artist presents 'a more emotionally-charged, more human figure of the Virgin, who now seems less like the unmoving centre of a theological regime than the active expression of compassion and love, whether bestowed in her queenly or in her maternal guise' (Silver).

123

QUINTEN MASSYS (1465/6–1530)
The Virgin and Child Enthroned
130 × 86 cm, Musée Royaux des Beaux-Arts, Brussels

The major motif of the painting is the Christ Child reading the book held by the Virgin. The way Christ concentrates on this task while putting one hand up to his mouth and turning the page with the other is an engaging and carefully observed detail. The panel dates from c.1505, but it reveals Massys's 'archaizing' tendencies. The motif of the Christ Child reading is one that both Rogier van der Weyden (Museo del Prado, Madrid) and Jan van Eyck (the Ince Hall Madonna, National Gallery, Melbourne) had employed on previous occasions. The context of the Virgin and Child enthroned in an interior as the central regal image denotes the panel's use as a devotional icon. The sense of the Virgin and Child as a piece of sculpture specially brought to life for the viewer is derived from Rogier van der Weyden's example, whereas the quality of the dress with its ornate border and of the long tresses of hair have more in common with Jan van Eyck.

124

PAOLO VERONESE (1528–1588)
The Virgin and Child with the Young St John the Baptist, SS. Elizabeth and Catherine of Alexandria
102.9 × 156.8 cm, The Putnam Foundation Timken Art Gallery, San Diego, California

Dating from 1565–70, the painting is a fine example of Veronese's prodigious powers of seemingly effortless composition. The figures are spread expansively across the picture but, nonetheless, remain tightly interlocked by gesture and glance. The internal rhythms are slow and mellifluous, not dissimilar to the heavy rich brocades worn by the figures. St Catherine of Alexandria, seen from the back on the right of the composition, leans down towards the Christ Child who playfully reaches up perhaps to play with the beads in her hair. St John the Baptist meanwhile tugs at Christ's leg, while the Virgin watches. St Elizabeth, by contrast, on the left, is more pensive guarding the cradle. Behind her is the open sky which releases the eye and invests the design with a different spatial dimension. The rich warm colours, silvery tone, and soft highlights underscore the poetry implicit within this innocent scene.

125

TITIAN (TIZIANO VECELLIO) (c.1477–1576)
The Virgin and Child
75.6 × 63.2 cm, National Gallery, London

The style denotes that this is a very late painting, dating from the 1570s. Many of Titian's late canvases were brought to varying degrees of finish, partly as a result of his elaborate working process. How Titian executed such a picture as this *Virgin and Child* is recorded for us by a seventeenth-century Venetian writer, Marco Boschini, who discussed Titian's technique with the painter Palma Giovane. The artist 'used to sketch in his pictures with a great mass of colours which served, one might say, as a bed or base for the compositions he then had to construct . . . Having constructed these precious foundations, he used to turn his pictures to the wall and leave them there without looking at them, sometimes for several months. When he wanted to apply his brush again he would examine them with the utmost rigour, as if they were his mortal enemies, to see if he could find any faults . . . In this way, working on the figures and revising them, he brought them to the most perfect symmetry that the beauty of art and nature can reveal; and after he had done this, while the picture was drying, he would turn his hand to another and work on it in the same way. Thus he gradually covered those quintessential forms with living flesh, bringing them by many stages to a state in which they lacked only the breath of life. He never painted a figure all at once . . . But the final stage of his last retouching involved his moderating here and there the brightest highlights by rubbing them with his fingers, reducing the contrast with the middle tones and harmonizing one tone with another . . .'

126
DOMENICO TINTORETTO (c.1560–1635)
The Madonna of the Stars
92.7 × 72.7 cm, National Gallery of Art, Washington D.C.: the Ralph and Mary Booth Collection

Domenico Tintoretto spent many years working as an assistant to his father, Jacopo, whose style forms the basis of his own. Only recently has Domenico's real ability both as a portraitist and as a religious painter begun to be appreciated. His loose, bold style was of some consequence for the establishment of Baroque painting in Venice. *The Madonna of the Stars* was probably executed by Domenico while he was still in his father's studio, perhaps c.1580. The style is typical of the ebullient brushwork favoured by Tintoretto and the composition is definitely proto-Baroque, the Virgin and Child depicted far out in the firmament. At first the painting appears to be a fragment from a larger composition, but the canvas has apparently not been cut down. The provenance of the picture provides no clue as to how it was originally displayed.

127
EL GRECO (DOMENIKOS THEOTOCOPOULOS)
(1541–1614)
The Holy Family with St Anne (detail)
138 × 103.5 cm, Svepmůvészeti Museum (Museum of Fine Arts), Budapest

The painting once formed part of a large-scale altarpiece in the church of the hospital of St John the Baptist Extra Muros, Toledo. The altarpiece is a composite of architecture, sculpture and painting, commissioned from El Greco in 1608. The artist had in fact been involved with the high altar of the church from 1595, but the contract for the whole complex including the lateral altar was not drawn up until a few years later. In fact, he failed to complete the work before his death and the project was completed by Jorge Manuel who made several modifications before his own death in 1630. The various parts of the altarpieces are now dispersed and the constituent elements known only from inventories. The style of *The Holy Family with St Anne* is in El Greco's later manner. The figures are seen from below and are notable for their bulbous shapes and elongated features. The treatment of colour adds to the emotional pitch of the work: the rose-red and blue of the Virgin's costume is seen

against the blue and white sky counteracting the orange of St Anne's dress.

128
AGOSTINO CARRACCI (1557–1602)
The Virgin and Child with the Young St John the Baptist and SS. Nicholas, Cecilia and Margaret
153 × 120 cm, Galleria Nazionale di Parma

Painted for the Benedictine convent of San Paolo in Parma and dated 1586, this altarpiece is in Agostino Carracci's early style. The debt to Correggio is adumbrated in the handling of the two female saints and the young St John. This last figure looks outwards over his shoulder to face the viewer while pointing to the Virgin and Child: he acts, therefore, as an intercessor. One of the advantages of this altarpiece is that it reveals Agostino Carracci's own stylistic characteristics which are most evident in the physiognomy and sharp illumination of the Virgin's face. So often overshadowed by the achievement of his younger brother, Annibale, it is too easily forgotten how good a painter Agostino could be. He was also a prolific print-maker.

129
ANTHONY VAN DYCK (1599–1641)
The Virgin and Child
64.1 × 49.5 cm, The Metropolitan Museum of Art, New York. Fletcher Fund

It is generally agreed that the painting was done while van Dyck was in Italy (1621–27), and, indeed, the poses recall the late *Virgin and Child* by Titian in the National Gallery, London. The paint surface is very thin, and technically the picture is unfinished. It seems that the outlines of the figures were traced from a cartoon or drawing, for there are indentations in the panel itself. The background is only sketched in, to offset the Virgin and Child, whose faces are modelled with care, while the draperies are broadly laid in with wonderfully fluid brushstrokes.

130
ANTHONY VAN DYCK (1599–1641)
The Virgin and Child with St Catherine of Alexandria
109.2 × 90.8 cm, The Metropolitan Museum of Art, New York. Bequest of Lilian S. Timken

Dating from c.1630, the painting was undertaken by van Dyck at the height of his powers during the second Antwerp period (1627–32), when the artist had returned to Antwerp after an extensive visit to Italy. This painting reflects van Dyck's absorption of works by Titian, Veronese, Parmigianino and Correggio, especially in the handling of paint. The composition is particularly clever in the use of diagonals to focus attention on the Christ Child. The group is placed beside an apple tree and a rose bush. The apple normally symbolizes the Fall of Man, but in this context is a reference to Salvation as in the verse in the *Song of Solomon* (8:5): 'I raised thee up under the apple tree.' The rose is the symbol of the Virgin: 'I am the rose of Sharon, and the lily of the valleys' (*Song of Solomon* 2:1), but also of the Passion of Christ and the Virgin's sorrow at her Son's fate.

131
JUSEPE DE RIBERA (1591–1652)
The Holy Family with SS. Anne and Catherine of Alexandria
209.6 × 154.3 cm, The Metropolitan Museum of Art, New York. Samuel D. Lee Fund

The canvas is signed and dated 1648. The subject is actually the Mystic Marriage of St Catherine. Born into the royal house of Alexandria, Catherine refused to marry and on being baptised dreamed that the Christ Child took her as his celestial spouse, placing a ring on her finger which she then discovered on awakening and kept. Eventually she suffered death by martyrdom. This is the only occasion on which Ribera painted the theme, and in so doing he created a late masterpiece. The picture dazzles by its powerful colouring, particularly of the Virgin's draperies. St Catherine has a refined beauty, wearing an elegant silver gown, white mantle and transparent veil that has slipped on to her shoulders. The composition is simply organized and is dependent upon an inverted triangle. Ribera does not allow the design to become static, however: at the moment of the mystical union a series of glances and movements enlivens the event — Christ looks at St Catherine, the Virgin looks at the viewer, St Joseph peers out from the gloom, St Anne approaches with a basket of fruit and holds a rose, the symbol of Christ's Passion. The artist cleverly fuses all of these fleeting actions into a single dazzling image.

132
MICHELANGELO MERISI DA CARAVAGGIO
(1571–1610)
The Madonna of Loreto
260 × 150 cm, San Agostino, Rome

This is one of Caravaggio's most important altarpieces. Painted in 1604/5 for the Cavaletti chapel in the church of San Agostino, Rome, it is still *in situ*. It represents a particularly dramatic treatment of the subject. The Madonna of Loreto was originally a sculptured group in the Santa Casa at Loreto which attracted pilgrims because it was believed to be the Virgin's actual home transported from the Holy Land. Caravaggio brings the Virgin and Child to life as if in answer to the prayers offered by the pilgrims seen kneeling in the foreground. The artist here implies that the miraculous appearance of the Virgin — an occurrence emphasized by her balletic pose — is the reward for faith. Furthermore, and at the time controversially, Caravaggio chose simple peasants as his pilgrims, whose worn clothes and skin are depicted with the utmost fidelity. The sharply foreshortened composition means that the visitor to the chapel shares the same viewpoint as the pilgrims, and therefore has an identical relationship with the Virgin and Child. Caravaggio makes dramatic use of the diagonal in the altarpiece and equally so of a bright light that is intensified by the dark background.

133
LAVINIA FONTANA (1552–1614)
The Virgin Adoring the Sleeping Child
Museum of Fine Arts, Boston

Lavinia Fontana was the daughter of the Bolognese artist Prospero Fontana (1512–1597). The father worked in Genoa for Perino del Vaga, a follower of Raphael, and then assisted Giorgio Vasari in Rome and Florence. His style was basically Mannerist, but he later rejected this for a more naturalistic style which his daughter inherited. This painting is a fresco fragment. The sprawling attitude of the sleeping Christ Child is a clear reference to the Pietà theme.

134
DOMENICO FETTI (c.1589–1623)
The Virgin and Child with SS. Catherine of Alexandria, Peter Martyr and Dominic (The Mystic Marriage of St Catherine)
229.5 × 140.5 cm, Kunsthistorisches Museum, Vienna

The Christ Child is shown putting the ring on the saint's finger. Two of the leading saints of the Dominican Order (SS. Dominic on the left and Peter Martyr on the right) witness the event. Because of this strong Dominican representation the painting is presumed to have hung originally in a church belonging to that Order. Fetti was born in Rome, where he was trained by Lodovico Cigoli and was influenced by Caravaggesque painters. In 1613 he was appointed court painter to the Gonzaga court in Mantua and so met Rubens. He was also able to absorb the best of Venetian art from the paintings that he saw in the Gonzaga collection. Fetti's works in Mantua, therefore, blended Roman and Venetian stylistic features. It is to this phase of his working life that *The Mystic Marriage of St Catherine* belongs.

135
BARTOLOMÉ ESTEBAN MURILLO (1617/18–1682)
The Virgin and Child
165.7 × 109.2 cm, The Metropolitan Museum of Art, New York. Rogers Fund

This painting, which dates from the 1570s and is therefore a relatively late work, is not unrelated to the composition of *The Virgin and Child in an Evening Landscape* executed by Titian (c.1562–65), formerly in the Escorial (now in the Alte Pinakothek, Munich). Murillo's feathery brushwork, opalescent colour and soft lights were admirably suited to the theme of *The Virgin and Child*, which he painted on numerous occasions. There is an intimacy and tenderness about these images that other painters could rarely equal.

136
GIOVANNI BATTISTA TIEPOLO (1696–1770)
The Madonna of the Goldfinch
63.2 × 50.2 cm, National Gallery of Art, Washington D.C.: the Samuel H. Kress Collection

This intimate Virgin and Child forms a contrast with the spectacularly ambitious compositions that dominate Tiepolo's oeuvre. Seen slightly from below, the Christ Child stares straight back at the viewer engaging our attention directly. Tiepolo's latent dynamism is apparent, however, in the way the Virgin's head and shoulders are positioned at a slight angle to the picture plane. There is an element almost of portraiture in the way the figures are brought so close to us, and there is considerable subtlety, too, in the suggestion of diagonals that never quite seem to solidify into a geometric pattern. The bright tones and fluent brushwork are the essence of Tiepolo's style.

The Deposition & Pietà

137
SIMONE MARTINI (c.1284–1344)
The Entombment
23.7 × 16.7 cm, Gemäldegalerie Staatliche Museen Preussischer Kulturbesitz, Berlin

There are a number of related panels: *The Annunciant Angel* and *The Annunciate Virgin* (both in Antwerp), *The Carrying of the Cross* (Paris), *The Crucifixion* (Antwerp), *The Descent from the Cross* (Antwerp). It is likely that these panels formed part of an elaborate altarpiece with folding wings (known as the Passion Polyptych). *The Carrying of the Cross* has on the back the coat-of-arms of the Orsini family, and it is almost certain that the altarpiece was commissioned by Cardinal Napoleone Orsini who died in Avignon in 1342. Since Simone Martini moved to Avignon c.1340, it is possible that he undertook the work in that city, but it may equally be that Cardinal Orsini had commissioned the altarpiece earlier and took it with him to Avignon. The matter is still eagerly debated. Although a close follower of Duccio, Simone Martini was also influenced by Giotto. The scenes of the Passion Polyptych combine both these stylistic traditions, particularly in the panel of *The Entombment*. Ranged on diagonals are numerous mourners surrounding Christ's body before it is lowered into the sarcophagus. Some of the figures are identifiable: the Virgin holds the body; St John the Evangelist is on the far right, his face hidden in his mantle; St Mary Magdalen is in the centre, her arms outstretched towards the body; Joseph of Arimathea anoints the feet, while Nicodemus holds the ointment. The rest of the company comprises female mourners and other disciples. The composition is memorable for the outpouring of grief expressed by the tearing of hair, the wild gesticulations, and the open mouths. The panel is small, and so the emotional tension created by all these people is very dramatic. Nothing, however, is more eloquent than the grief expressed by those who sit with their backs to the viewer.

138
DUCCIO DI BUONINSEGNA (active 1278–1318/9)
The Deposition from the Cross
50 × 53.7 cm, Museo dell' Opera della Metropolitana, Siena

Scenes from Christ's Passion occur on the back of Duccio's vast two-sided altarpiece known as the Maestà, painted between 1308 and 1311 for the cathedral in Siena. *The Deposition from the Cross* was one of the scenes placed to the side of the double panel of *The Crucifixion*, which was situated on the central axis. As with many of the narrative scenes on the Maestà, Duccio used Byzantine iconographical sources. In *The Deposition* he shows the Virgin reaching up and kissing Christ's face as the body slumps forward. The arrangement of the figures is beautifully controlled by the clever exploitation of diagonal, vertical and horizontal lines. The touching sentiment expressed by the action of the Virgin as she kisses Christ is forcefully countered by the grim necessity for the removal of the nails attaching the feet to the Cross. The way Nicodemus lowers the body of Christ — supporting his weight by hooking his

arm over the bar of the Cross — is also an evocative passage. Even though the subject was often painted in Italy during the fifteenth and early sixteenth centuries, the directness and simplicity of Duccio's panel is not surpassed.

139
ROGIER VAN DER WEYDEN (1399/1400–1464)
The Deposition from the Cross
220 × 262 cm, Museo del Prado, Madrid

It is believed that this famous and influential altarpiece was painted by Rogier van der Weyden for the chapel of the Crossbowmen's Guild in the church of Notre Dame-hors-les-Murs at Louvain. It is the starting point for the study of the oeuvre of the artist and was painted shortly before 1443. By 1574 the altarpiece was recorded in the Escorial when it was reported to have had folding shutters. The composition was frequently copied and adapted during the late fifteenth and early sixteenth centuries. It was engraved by the Master of the Banderoles (active c.1450–70) and in the sixteenth century by Michael Coxcie. The composition was also known in Italy where Fra Angelico shows some knowledge of it in his altarpiece of the *Deposition* painted for S. Trinita, Florence (c.1443). The figures are arranged as in a tableau. Although they are placed on natural ground, they are enclosed within a gilt niche. The principal figure is Christ whose body is set on a diagonal as he is lowered from the cross. Significantly, the Virgin's body, falling to the ground in a faint, is placed on a similar diagonal. She is supported by St John the Evangelist and the two Maries. Mary Magdalen is on the opposite side, her body literally contorted by grief and her hands clasped together in a gesture of despair. The two standing men are Joseph of Arimathaea, holding Christ's body under the arms, and Nicodemus, holding the legs. The altarpiece is notable for the paradox between the despair displayed by the figures and the restraint used to represent emotion. The emphasis is very much on drawing expressive of shape and pattern, rather than on colour or realism. It is a majestic work, beautifully observed and brilliantly executed, underscored by an undeniable feeling of spirituality.

140
COLYN DE COTER (c.1455–1538/9)
The Deposition from the Cross
109 × 83.5 cm, Staatsgalerie, Stuttgart

The artist was a follower of Hugo van der Goes. Although he was registered in the Antwerp Guild in 1493, he came from Brussels and it was there that he was for the most part active. His paintings carry on the tradition of Rogier van der Weyden and Hugo van der Goes in so far as he was dependent upon their compositions, but stylistically, Colyn de Coter was subject to the influence of Mannerism, in which style he often reinterpreted the designs of his distinguished predecessors. This panel was originally rounded at the top and only later were pieces added to give it a rectangular format. The composition is often described as being after a lost work by either Rogier van der Weyden or Hugo van der Goes, but it seems more likely that the artist devised it himself and he appears to have reused it on other occasions. The composition is notable for its mosaic of forms and for its compressed emotion. The visual effect is like a fan opening, whereas geometrically the design is based on a series of diagonals: Nicodemus and Joseph of Arimathea are at the top, Christ below, then St John the Evangelist, and finally the Virgin. The figures are placed so as to portray a crescendo of grief extending downwards from Nicodemus. Friedländer wrote of Colyn de Coter, 'In the dim lighting of churches, his altar panels impressed with their massiveness, their air of doom, the juxtaposition of tall column-like figures. He was little concerned with spatial depth and landscape, placing his characters in the foremost level and filling the foreground with a dense wall of figures.'

141
ROGIER VAN DER WEYDEN (c.1400–1464)
The Pietà
32.2 × 47.2 cm, Musées Royaux des Beaux-Arts, Brussels

This composition exists in several versions emanating from the workshop of Rogier van der Weyden (c.1450) in which the figures chosen for representation vary. Unlike the acknowledged autograph painting of *The Pietà* in the National Gallery, London, this picture concentrates more vividly on the figures who fill the foreground and are silhouetted against the sky. The Virgin supports the upper part of Christ's body while the legs rest on the ground; St John the Evangelist assists the Virgin; St Mary Magdalen grieves over the body, her hands clasped together. A landscape stretches behind the figures; the skull of Adam, signifying Golgotha, is by Christ's feet. 'Rogier's creatures are sensitive to pain, they suffer, but they suffer with dignity. Sorrow has etched their features, bent their stature, stiffened or convulsed their limbs. Pain, resisted with body and soul, is the dramatic driving-force behind these upward-striving humans' (Friedländer).

142
GERARD DAVID (active c.1484–1523)
The Pietà
80 × 50 cm, Oskar Reinhart Collection, Winterthur

The picture is a version of the centre panel of the artist's altarpiece of *The Lamentation* now divided between the John G. Johnson Collection at the Philadelphia Museum of Art, and the Lehman Collection in the Metropolitan Museum of Art, New York. *The Lamentation* in the centre of the original altarpiece was flanked by scenes of *Christ Carrying the Cross* and *The Resurrection*; *The Annunciation* was painted on the back of the shutters and therefore visible only when closed. The panel in Philadelphia includes the figures of St John the Evangelist and Mary Magdalen. Here they are omitted so that the Virgin kneels alone, cradling the body of her Son before the landscape. The sense of desolation is given greater poignancy as a result of isolating the figures to make a separate composition; the grief is made palpable by the surrounding silence.

143
ATTRIBUTED TO ENGUERRAND QUARTON (active 1444–1466)
The Pietà
163 × 218.5 cm, Musée du Louvre, Paris

This famous panel originally came from the Hospice of Villeneuve-les-Avignon and is in all probability the work of a Provençal painter c.1460. There has been much discussion about the exact attribution, although the name of Enguerrand Quarton is often suggested. Christ lies on the Virgin's lap; St John the Evangelist supports the head, and St Mary Magdalen holds a jar of ointment at the feet. The Virgin's hands are folded in prayer while St Mary Magdalen weeps. The kneeling donor on the left has yet to be identified. Behind him is a city balancing the landscape on the right. The painting is one of the masterpieces of fifteenth-century French art, partly on account of the skill with which it is executed, but also partly because of its emotional impact derived from the unusual internal rhythms and realistic drawing. The composition is built upon a slow rising curve echoed by the position of Christ's body. The expressions reflect the stark horror of the occasion. Grete Ring wrote, 'It is indeed one of the great masterpieces of the epoch, but its author appears to be timeless as well as nameless. The composition has the severe simplicity of great sculpture, the figures arranged on one plane, in the manner of high relief, their majestic silhouettes standing out from the "archaic" gold background. All details and accessories are eliminated, the interest focused on the simple rhythmical movement of the group. The deep and austere colours enhance the effect of suffering and sadness.'

144
GIOVANNI BELLINI (c.1430–1516)
The Pietà
87 × 107 cm, Pinacoteca di Brera, Milan

Christ stands in the tomb, supported by the Virgin on the left and St John the Evangelist on the right. These figures are conceived on a monumental scale, and are set in the immediate foreground against an intricately painted landscape that includes a river in the middle distance and a view of Jerusalem. The most eloquent part of the background, however, is the sky, which is streaked with soft rose-red tints. The sense of sorrow that dominates the picture is derived partly from the way in which the mood of the landscape matches the subject. Similarly, Bellini concentrates on muted colours using two different shades of blue and a subdued red for the draperies, offset by a grey pallor of the flesh tones. There is a marked contrast between the close physical proximity of the Virgin's face to Christ's body, now drained of life, and St John's more distant relationship. The style of the painting has been described as 'the fullest development and most perfect expression of Giovanni's earlier manner', which implies a date towards the end of the 1460s when he began to put less emphasis on line and more on modelling. The picture probably had a special significance for the artist, since he has added a Latin couplet along the lower edge in the centre which reads, 'When these swelling eyes evoke groans, this [very] work of Giovanni Bellini could shed tears'. The most poignant element in this Pietà is the characterization of the Virgin and St John. 'There is no over-emphasis of the drama of grief

here, but a deeply restrained rendering of the beauty of sorrow that makes this one of the great classic achievements of European art.' (Robertson)

145
DIERIC BOUTS (active 1457, died 1475)
Mater Dolorosa
37 × 28 cm, The Art Institute of Chicago. Chester D. Tripp Endowment Fund

The theme of the *Mater Dolorosa* involves the single figure of the Virgin grieving at the death of Christ, who is often depicted as the Man of Sorrows on an accompanying panel, so forming a diptych. There are many versions from the Bouts workshop. It is not a narrative subject but one that is meant to inspire compassion, and Bouts had the perfect skills for this theme, since his figures slip so easily between the spheres of idealism and realism. The firm outline of the Virgin is achieved with great economy as a simple form against a plain background, but the swollen red eyes, the tears and the hands are painted with great attention to detail. Such naturalism, however, does not detract from the gentle demeanour that characterizes this powerful yet moving depiction of the sorrowing Virgin personifying the Church in a troubled world.

146
ERCOLE DE' ROBERTI (active 1479–1496)
The Pietà
34.3 × 31.3 cm, Walker Art Gallery, Liverpool

There is some evidence to show that the panel formed part of the main altarpiece in the church of San Giovanni in Monte, Bologna, but the exact arrangement of the various works described as once having been on the main altar is uncertain. It is known, however, that *The Pietà* was accompanied by two other panels, *The Betrayal of Christ* and *The Way to Calvary*, also by Ercole and now in Dresden. The figure of the grieving Virgin — who has a pronounced grimace on her face — is characteristic of Emilian painting of the last quarter of the fifteenth century. The Virgin cradles the dead Christ on her lap; His limbs are attenuated as a result of the process of death by crucifixion. The scene of Calvary acts as a backdrop behind the figure. The viewer is immediately struck by the barrenness of the landscape, by the isolation of the Virgin and her Son, and by the feeling of loss. It is a moment of private grief, but one that has universal significance. The head of the dead Christ is a memorable passage of painting. Ercole de' Roberti worked in Ferrara and Bologna. He was the pupil of Cosimo Tura and became court artist to the Este family in Ferrara from 1487 to 1494. His art has considerable vitality and his frescoes (now destroyed, apart from a single fragment) in the Garganelli chapel in San Pietro, Bologna, were admired by Michelangelo amongst others.

147
SANDRO BOTTICELLI (1445–1510)
The Pietà
110 × 207 cm, Alte Pinakothek, Munich

The picture was originally in the church of San Paolino, Florence, near where Botticelli lived, and dates from the early 1490s. The compositional emphasis is on the horizontal: the central figures lean outwards in different directions, so that the eye is led to the very edges of the painting. The body of Christ is the focus of attention — even though it is lifeless and limp. The Virgin, St John the Evangelist, Mary Magdalen and two holy women attend the body, while SS. Jerome and Paul (to the left) and St Peter (to the right) look on. The vibrant colours form a contrast with the alabaster flesh tones of the dead Christ and help to define the positions of the figure in relation to the dark interior of the tomb before which the scene takes place. The painting is not unlike an elegy in mood. It is one of Botticelli's most poignant works, even though it lacks the emotional impact of *The Pietà* in Milan. There is still a sense here that the artist is more interested in pattern as opposed to the depiction of soul-searching anguish.

148
SANDRO BOTTICELLI (1445–1510)
The Pietà
107 × 71 cm, Museo Poldi-Pezzoli, Milan

The picture originally hung on one of the pillars in the church of Santa Maria Maggiore in Florence, where it was seen by Vasari in the sixteenth century. It is a late work by Botticelli, dating from the 1490s when he evolved a highly personal and emotionally charged style, perhaps as a consequence of the preaching of the Dominican monk, Girolamo Savonarola. Aspects of Botticelli's late style anticipate Florentine Mannerist art of the 1520s, particularly the contorted poses and impassioned gestures. The composition of this *Pietà* is based upon a series of interlocking forms. The dead Christ lies across the Virgin's lap while she herself is supported by St John the Evangelist. The Magdalen anoints Christ's feet with her tears, and another female figure cradles his head. To the left yet another female figure hides her face in grief. Joseph of Arimathea holds the crown of thorns and the nails at the back by the tomb. Botticelli forms all of these various shapes into a circular pattern that resembles a coiled spring. The tension in the composition matches the emotional content of the picture. As such, Botticelli's painting is far removed from the young Michelangelo's sculptured *Pietà* in St Peter's, Rome, which was carved during this same decade. It is closer to Pontormo's fresco of *The Deposition* in the church of Santa Felicità, Florence, painted c.1526–28.

149
TITIAN (TIZIANO VECELLIO) (c.1477–1576)
The Pietà
353 × 348 cm, Galleria dell' Accademia, Venice

The Pietà is placed within a niche flanked by statues of Moses to the left and the Hellespontine Sibyl, who prophesied the death of Christ, on the right. The artist himself appears in the guise of the penitent St Jerome, kneeling before the dead Christ and the Virgin. The half-dome over the niche is adorned with an image of the pelican feeding her young with her own blood, a symbol of Christ's crucifixion. This sacramental theme is underscored by the torch-bearing angel and by the spluttering candles on the pediment of the niche. The main thrust of the composition is the diagonal extending from St Jerome to the figure of Mary Magdalen moving out of the composition with her right arm raised — a pose that is quoted from antique sarcophagi. The painting is a very late work by Titian, for whom the subject most probably had a profound personal

significance. It is datable to the year in which the artist died, and was in fact finished by Palma Giovane, as recorded in an inscription at the lower edge. The conception and most of the creation, however, are certainly Titian's. The impressionistic brushwork and subdued colouring are typical of the painter's late works.

150
ANNIBALE CARRACCI (1560–1609)
The Pietà
156 × 149 cm, Museo e Gallerie di Capodimonte, Naples

The composition takes as its point of departure Michelangelo's famous sculpture in St Peter's, Rome, and Correggio's painting of the theme in Parma. Probably commissioned by Cardinal Odoardo Farnese in c.1599/1600, Carracci's *Pietà* has been universally admired since the day it was executed. Posner has written, 'In the Naples *Pietà* beauty of form and expressive gesture combine to produce one of the great masterpieces of European art around 1600. A pyramid of three figures, brightly lit and isolated in the dark night, is set against the cold stone blocks of the tomb at the right. Christ's body, perfect in form and astonishingly graceful in the relaxation of death, rests against the Madonna's thigh. With a majestic, funereal rhythm the composition rises from the head of Christ to the head of His mother — their regular, "sculptured" features set for eternity in death and grief — and descends to the Madonna's hand, open in a gesture of appeal and despair, and on to Christ's right hand, hanging limply and held by a *putto*. The *putto* turns to look at his companion, who closes the dirge with a final cry of horror as he touches a sharp spike of the Crown of Thorns.'

151
JUSEPE DE RIBERA (1591–1652)
The Pietà
157 × 210 cm, Thyssen-Bornemisza Collection, Lugano

Although born in Spain, Ribera went to Italy in 1611 and, after studying the works of Correggio in Parma and Lodovico Carracci in Bologna, moved to Rome where he was deeply influenced by Caravaggio. The rich colouring, the tenebrist treatment of light, and the constant recourse to naturalism in order to heighten religious effect are aspects taken from Caravaggio that form the basis of Ribera's style. He painted the theme of the Pietà several times, but this is his earliest known attempt at the subject and dates from 1633. Here the artist gives the composition a pronounced horizontal emphasis. Surrounding the body of Christ are the Virgin, St John the Evangelist, Joseph of Arimathea at the head, and Mary Magdalen kissing the feet. The orange, blue, red and green chord of colour is one often employed by Ribera. The faces of the Virgin and St John the Evangelist are sharply illuminated by light that seems to be reflected from Christ's body. The Virgin's pleading gesture and anxious look upwards sets the emotional tone of the picture.

The Death, Assumption & Coronation of the Virgin

152
DUCCIO DI BUONINSEGNA (active 1278–1318/19)
The Funeral of the Virgin
58 × 52.5 cm, Museo dell' Opera del Duomo, Siena

Although there is a difference in shape from the other panels by Duccio recounting the last days of the Virgin from the Maestà included here, this panel does form part of that sequence. While the other panels have been cut down into a rectangular format, *The Funeral of the Virgin* has retained its original gabled edges. The apostles are shown carrying the body of the Virgin on a bier before the walls of Jerusalem. The octagonal building in the background (not unlike a Baptistery in design) may be a representation of the Temple in Jerusalem: Duccio also includes it in the background of the depiction of *Christ entering Jerusalem* on the back of the Maestà. An interesting episode recounted in *The Golden Legend* is incorporated by Duccio in *The Funeral of the Virgin*. The woman following the bier on the left is called Salome. She apparently doubted the Immaculate Conception and her hands were shrivelled as a punishment. The only cure was to touch the Virgin's bier which she is shown doing in this panel. The pose is very probably derived from a figure occurring on an antique sarcophagus of Medea. Interestingly, *The Funeral of the Virgin* was backed on the Maestà by *The Incredulity of St Thomas* — another representation of disbelief.

153
DUCCIO DI BUONINSEGNA (active 1278–1318/19)
The Apostles' Farewell to the Virgin
41.5 × 54 cm, Museo dell' Opera della Metropolitana, Siena

The high altarpiece known as the Maestà was painted by Duccio for the cathedral in Siena between 1308 and 1311: on completion the panel was carried through the streets of Siena before being installed as the high altarpiece in the cathedral. It was painted on both sides. Around the main image of *The Virgin and Child enthroned with Saints* there was placed a large number of narrative scenes illustrating the last days of the Virgin and the life of Christ. These narrative scenes begin on the front and extend on to the back, where they fill the whole panel. An enormous project, the Maestà is the greatest area of narrative painting on panel achieved in Italy during the fourteenth century. *The Apostles' Farewell to the Virgin* formed part of the sequence recounting the last days of the Virgin which filled the front pinnacles of the altarpiece above the Virgin and Child enthroned with Saints. The predella of the front side was devoted to the infancy of Christ, so that the overall purpose of the side facing the congregation in the cathedral was to praise the Virgin. The scenes of the last days of the Virgin conform with the literary description in *The Golden Legend* of Jacobus de Voragine, although they were at this date more commonly depicted in Byzantine art. Interestingly, because of the sequence of the narrative Duccio often had to repeat many of the interiors in which the scenes are set in order to retain a sense of unity of time and place. The interior shown here, for example, occurs three times in this section of the altarpiece.

DUCCIO DI BUONINSEGNA (active 1278–1318/19)
The Burial of the Virgin
41.2 × 54 cm, Museo dell' Opera della
Metropolitana, Siena

This is another scene from the panels depicting the last days of the Virgin placed in the pinnacles on the front side of Duccio's Maestà (1308/1311). *The Burial of the Virgin Mary* is shown in a landscape; the apostles are in attendance. The landscape is less desolate than that used by Duccio for *The Entombment of Christ* on the back of the Maestà. It is typical of Duccio's sophisticated linear style that the downwards curve of the landscape is counteracted by the rising curve made by the row of the apostles' heads as they stoop over the Virgin's body. Similarly, the verticals formed by the trees balance the pronounced horizontal emphasis in the foreground.

155

PIETER BRUEGEL THE ELDER (c.1525/30–1569)
The Death of the Virgin
36 × 54.5 cm, Upton House, Banbury

The painting is executed in grisaille, which makes the representation of the different lighting effects within this interior scene a major technical feat and, furthermore, one that anticipates Rembrandt. The picture was painted for Bruegel's friend, the geographer Abraham Ortelius, who lived in Antwerp, most probably c.1564. As in many of Bruegel's paintings, he uses the occasion to make a comment on his own time. *The Death of the Virgin* emphasizes that the just will be saved. Following the account given by Jacobus de Voragine in *The Golden Legend*, Bruegel sees the Virgin's death as a public event attended not only by the apostles, but by a whole throng of people. The bed is situated in the upper right corner of the composition. Some onlookers gather round, while others press forward into the room. The rest of the room is left empty, apart from a solitary figure asleep by the fire where a cat can also be seen. The table in the centre foreground is piled high with abandoned plates and jugs. The contrast between the two parts of the room heightens the sense of occasion, just as the light behind the Virgin's head and the bulbous awning suspended from the top of the bed focus attention on the principal figure.

156

MICHELANGELO MERISI DA CARAVAGGIO
(1571–1610)
The Death of the Virgin
369 × 245 cm, Musée du Louvre, Paris

The painting is extremely large, and was commissioned in 1604/5 by a papal lawyer, Laerzio Cherubini, for his chapel in the church of Santa Maria della Scala, Rome. It is one of Caravaggio's most moving compositions, not least for the realistic representation of the Virgin who has one arm extended outwards and the other lying across her stomach. As so often with Caravaggio, the design operates on the basis of a diagonal. The figures nearest to the body register profound grief, but even this emotion is expressed directly. 'Like late paintings by Rembrandt, *The Death of the Virgin* seems full of emotion conveyed by bulky, numbed bodies that are too overwhelmed by their feelings to

express them' (Hibbard). It was apparently said at the time that Caravaggio's model for the young Virgin in the scene was a whore who was the artist's mistress. As a result, the picture was immediately rejected by the church of Santa Maria della Scala, and critics also found fault with the bare legs and swollen form of the dead Virgin. The problem was that Caravaggio showed the figure motionless in death, as opposed to dying, and on that hung a theological issue. Today the painting moves us because of its faithful depiction of death. Rubens much admired the altarpiece when he was in Rome (1605–8), and through him it was sold to the Duke of Mantua in 1607, from where it entered the collections of Charles I of England and Louis XIV of France.

157

ANDREA DEL CASTAGNO (1417/19–1457)
The Assumption of the Virgin with SS. Julian and Miniatus
131 × 150.5 cm, Gemäldegalerie Staatliche Museen Preussischer Kulturbesitz, Berlin

Andrea del Castagno painted this panel in 1450 for the church of San Miniato fra le Torri, Florence. The inclusion of St Miniatus on the right is accounted for because he is the titular saint of the church. Castagno's *Assumption of the Virgin* is a major feat in the depiction of levitation, for here it seems as though the Virgin really does rise upwards in the air. This is not a symbolic representation, but an attempt to show a body ascending from earth into heaven — in short, an experiment in transforming a miraculous event into a realistic one. The saints, however, observe the Assumption somewhat non-chalantly and it is the four angels who are more convincing in their role as bearers hovering between the tomb and the sky. Their athletic twisted bodies, wind-blown garments and flying locks, are unmistakably the work of Castagno. Vasari referred to these angels as being executed 'in a manner not done until this time', simply because they define the space they inhabit. The hot palette favoured by the artist supplements the daring innovations of this altarpiece.

158

TITIAN (TIZIANO VECELLIO) (c.1477–1576)
The Assumption of the Virgin
690 × 360 cm, Santa Maria dei Frari, Venice

Titian's Frari altarpiece (1516–18) is one of the most celebrated works in the history of European art. Seen on the main altar from the end of a long nave, the energy of the composition, and the warmth of its colour, is immediately and effectively apparent. The artist injects dynamism into a subject that had been treated rather literally or unimaginatively by his predecessors, and so invests the scene with a memorable sense of drama. Titian divides the painting roughly into two halves: the apostles are below, and the Virgin, surrounded by angels and cherubs, ascends towards God the Father at the top of the composition. The painter has depicted the actual moment of the Assumption. The Virgin's arms are outstretched in a gesture of faith; below, the apostles raise their arms in incredulity. The effect of the altarpiece is greatly enhanced by the colour. The Virgin and some of the apostles are in red robes complemented by green and white draperies. The figures are set against a pale-blue sky that changes to

a gold light higher up the altarpiece. Titian's *Assumption of the Virgin* is often compared with the major works of Raphael and Michelangelo. The altarpiece firmly established Titian's reputation in Venice.

159

EL GRECO (DOMENIKOS THEOTOCOPOULOS)
(1541–1614)
The Assumption of the Virgin
301.3 × 228.7 cm, The Art Institute of Chicago, Gift of Nancy Atwood Sprague in memory of Albert Arnold Sprague

This exceedingly tall and powerfully conceived painting was the high altarpiece of the newly built church of Santo Domingo el Antiguo, Toledo. It was commissioned with funds bequeathed by Doña Maria de Silva who had been lady-in-waiting to the Empress Isabella, wife of Charles V. The altarpiece is dated 1577 and was part of a substantial scheme of decoration in the sanctuary of the church, the success of which made El Greco's reputation in Spain. The main stylistic terms of reference, however, are Italian; the artist had just returned to Spain after a period of ten years or so in Venice and Rome. A source of inspiration was undoubtedly Titian's altarpiece of the *Assumption* in the church of the Frari, Venice, but the tall, spiralling, gesturing figures are more akin to those of Tintoretto, while the colour contrasts are comparable with Veronese. The pronounced vertical axis may have been imposed upon the artist, but it also suited the Mannerist tendencies that he had absorbed from Roman art. There is, for instance, little recession into depth: the billowing draperies are flattened in the same way as the sarcophagus, which resembles a cardboard cut-out. The organization of the figures was dictated by the fact that the tabernacle containing the host extended right up into the main field of the altarpiece. To allow for this El Greco left a convenient space in the centre and balanced the figures on either side so that the apostle in the left foreground looks inwards, while the apostle in the right foreground faces outwards. In the original ensemble a representation of the *Trinity* was placed above the *Assumption*.

160

PAOLO and GIOVANNI VENEZIANO (active 1321–1358)
The Coronation of the Virgin
110 × 68.5 cm, The Frick Collection, New York

The theme of the Coronation of the Virgin was painted several times by Paolo Veneziano, and his compositions were much imitated in his own workshop and by his followers. This is his last dated (1358) work and is signed jointly with his son Giovanni. It is part of an altarpiece of which other sections are dispersed in various collections. The composition is stereotyped and follows a tradition that was in part dependent upon Byzantine art. The sun and moon beneath the feet of Christ and the Virgin are attributes based on biblical sources. The inscription along the base of the throne is from the Eastertide antiphon, 'Queen of Heaven rejoice, alleluia, for He whom thou didst deserve to bear, alleluia.' This outburst of praise Paolo Veneziano has represented literally with the angelic orchestra assembled above the pink marble throne. Venetian painters often represented *The Coronation of the Virgin* with a full orchestra, thus giving the moment itself a celestial context. The colour, too, is equally vivid — a confection of pink, white, blue, red and yellow.

161

MARIOTTO DI NARDO (recorded 1394–1431)
The Coronation of the Virgin
131.7 × 68.5 cm, The Minneapolis Institute of Arts

The Coronation of the Virgin was originally the centre panel of a large altarpiece commissioned by the Confraternity of the Virgin and St Stephen for the church of San Stefano al Ponte, Florence. The other elements of this altarpiece, which is dated 1408, are now dispersed in various collections. Mariotto di Nardo was a retardataire artist who maintained the tradition of the Orcagna workshop into the fifteenth century. Many of his compositions are dependent upon established formulae, but he was, nevertheless, an imposing and often convincing painter. There is a grandeur about this *Coronation of the Virgin* in its simple design. The Virgin and Christ are seated on a gabled marble throne at the base of which is a group of music-making angels. The positioning of these angels between the throne and the viewer successfully creates a feeling of recession within the composition. The main figures show little emotion and are seated stiffly on the marble throne, but the solemn and static visual effect that results is by no means inappropriate for the subject.

162

GENTILE DA FABRIANO (c.1370–1427)
The Coronation of the Virgin
158 × 79 cm, Pinacoteca di Brera, Milan

The scene of the *Coronation* is the central panel of a substantial altarpiece painted by Gentile da Fabriano for the church of Santa Maria di Valdisasso near Fabriano. On either side of the main panel were SS. Jerome and Francis (to the left) and SS. Dominic and Mary Magdalen (to the right). Above these figures, in smaller panels, were narrative depictions such as *St John the Baptist in the Desert* and *St Francis Receiving the Stigmata*. The original order of these panels was disturbed when the altarpiece was reframed in 1925. The work is Gentile da Fabriano's first masterpiece and dates from c.1410. Rhythm and colour dominate the design. The Virgin and Christ are suspended in mid-air against a gold background incised with tongues of fire. Above, in the apex of the panel, God the Father unites the Virgin and Christ; below, on the last circle of heaven, angels play musical instruments. Gentile da Fabriano relentlessly pursues perfection and beauty in this altarpiece: he consciously sets out to create a heavenly vision, and he succeeds not just by the attention given to exquisite details of texture and refinement, but by the contrast between the visionary aspects of the Coronation itself and the more naturalistic treatment of the other scenes. As a painter, Gentile da Fabriano is of some consequence. His style developed from those characteristics associated with the International Gothic style to works with broadly modelled figures and carefully articulated space that were admired by painters of the early Renaissance. He worked in Venice, Florence, Siena and Rome.

163

FRA ANGELICO (c.1395–1455)
The Coronation of the Virgin
209 × 206 cm, Musée du Louvre, Paris

This is one of Fra Angelico's largest works and was painted for the church of San Domenico, Fiesole, fairly late in the artist's life (c.1450). There is perhaps a compositional defect in that the viewer at first looks down on to the patterned floor, but then upwards towards the canopy under which the Coronation of the Virgin is taking place. All around on the steps and in the foreground are angels and saints witnessing the event. The composition is essentially circular. At the top of the circle are Christ and the Virgin. Fra Angelico has left a void in the centre, but on the vertical axis he isolates the jar held in Mary Magdalen's left hand: it is a moving and striking image — a moment of calm amidst all the fanfares and jubilation. The chief stylistic feature of the altarpiece is the range of colour and the decorative qualities of the brocades. The patterned floor and the marbled steps are a veritable kaleidoscope of colour that adds to the festive occasion. A number of the faces among the saints and angels are sharply individualized. There are few passages of such elegance in fifteenth-century Italian painting as the modelling of the drapery worn by the female saint kneeling in the lower right corner.

164

GIOVANNI BELLINI (c.1430–1516)
The Coronation of the Virgin
262 × 240 cm, Museo Civico, Pesaro

Giovanni Bellini's *Coronation of the Virgin* at Pesaro is a key work in any discussion of his development as an artist. It is, for instance, the earliest surviving example of a large-scale altarpiece by Bellini showing the figures grouped in a single area. There has, however, been considerable debate about the date of its execution, a matter that hinges on Bellini's relationship with Antonello de Messina. Everyone agrees that the altarpiece dates from the 1470s, but whether before or after 1475 is still in dispute. The composition has a low viewpoint: Bellini has had to overcome the difficulty of allowing the main protagonists to be seated while the subsidiary figures are shown standing. Furthermore, he has pierced the marble throne at the back so that the viewer espies a landscape with a hilltop fortress (the Sforza stronghold at Gradara) as though through a window. The monumental forms of the flanking saints (Paul, Peter, Jerome and Francis), the disposition of objects within three-dimensional space, and the diffusion of colours within a scene bathed in crystalline light, reveal the influence on Bellini of Piero della Francesca, who had been working at nearby Rimini at the beginning of the 1450s — a stylistic acknowledgement of the utmost significance for Italian art.

165

DIEGO VELÁZQUEZ (1599–1660)
The Coronation of the Virgin by the Trinity
176 × 124 cm, Museo del Prado, Madrid

Velázquez was a painter who could depict religious ecstasy with the same conviction that he brought to the secular sphere of portraits, *genre* or landscapes. *The Coronation of the Virgin* was painted for the Oratory of Queen Isabel of Bourbon, the wife of Philip IV, in her private apartments in the Alcázar, Madrid. The Queen died in 1644, and it is generally accepted that the painting dates from a short time before that year. The composition, partly derived from one by Rubens known through an engraving, is carefully balanced. Christ is on the left of the Virgin, and God the Father to the right: they hold a floral crown over the Virgin's head. The scene is bathed in a golden light emanating from the Holy Ghost in the form of a Dove. The draperies are also painted in warm hues of red, blue and mauve. Most striking of all, however, is the composure of the Virgin, expressed not only by the closed eyelids but also by the calm gesture made with the hands. There are other wonderful passages in the painting, such as the way the Virgin's drapery merges with the phosphorescent cloud near the lower edge, or the cherubim on the right seen *di sotto in su* helping to carry the Virgin upwards. The technical assurance in the execution of this painting reveals Velázquez's debt to Titian — but it would not be untenable to claim that he has improved upon the Venetian master.

Index of Painters

The plate numbers given below refer both to the illustrations and to the annotations to them (pages 222–245).

Author's Acknowledgments

I am very pleased to acknowledge the support of my publisher, Martin Heller, throughout the preparation of this book. I am also extremely grateful to Derek Birdsall, the book's ever more distinguished designer and to Christopher Lloyd who has contributed the notes on the plates. Derek Birdsall is always a great pleasure to work with as well as to watch working, and Christopher Lloyd has been as expertly industrious as he has. I consider it an honour that Peter Levi consented to write his very graceful introductory essay.

I would also like to thank Barbara Heller and Christina Weir who have taken so much trouble in obtaining the colour transparencies of the pictures as well as Rachel Duffield of Macdonald Orbis and Martyn Longly the Production Manager with whom it is a pleasure to inspect colour proofs — also Christopher Fagg who has energetically pulled everyone's contributions together. Several good friends have suggested pictures that I did not know of, and I would particularly thank Isobel Johnstone, Catherine Lampert and Alister Warman as well as Frank Auerbach, Michael Howard and Richard Kendall.

Among the very obliging people at the sources of the pictures I am most indebted to Ancilla Antonini of the Scala agency in Florence, Martha Wolff and Kristy Stewart of the Art Institute of Chicago, Jane Hankins of the Museum of Fine Art in Boston, Katharine Baetger and Deanna Cross of the Metropolitan Museum in New York and Beverley Brown and Ira Bartfield of the National Gallery in Washington. All galleries and agencies credited have been more than helpful.

Bruce Bernard